Great
War
Stories

D0814484

Rifleman Dodd
by C.S. Forester

The General
by C.S. Forester

Captain from Connecticut
by C.S. Forester

Fix Bayonets!
by John W. Thomason

Victory at High Tide
by Robert Debs Heinl

Soldiers of the Sea
by Robert Debs Heinl

The U.S. Marine Corps and Defense Unification 1944-47
by Gordon W. Keiser

"Boney" Fuller
by Anthony John Trythall

Fix Bayonets!

FIX BAYONETS!

Stories of World War I

by

John W. Thomason

Illustrated by the Author

The Nautical & Aviation Publishing Company of America
Charleston, South Carolina

First published in 1925 by Charles Scribner's Sons.
Foreword © 2007 by the Nautical & Aviation Publishing
Company of America Inc.,
2055 Middleburg Lane, Mount Pleasant, South Carolina
29464. All rights reserved.

Library of Congress Card Number: 2007930314

John W. Thomason

ISBN: 978-1-877853-69-2

Foreword by Merrill L. Bartlett,
Lieutenant Colonel, USMC (Ret.)

Capture of Blanc Mont Ridge
Cover painting by George M. Harding
Courtesy of the Navy Art Collection, Naval Historical
Center, Washington D.C.
Back cover and above photo of the author are official U.S. Navy

Printed in the United States of America
First Printing 2007

TO
THE MEN OF THE FIRST BATTALION
FIFTH REGIMENT
UNITED STATES MARINE CORPS
1918

TABLE OF CONTENTS

Foreword   xiii

Battle Sight   3

The Charge at Soissons   53

Marines at Blanc Mont   95

Monkey-Meat   142

The Rhine   159

List of Illustrations

Occasional wounded Frenchmen drifted back   5

Sketches from Captain Thomason's note-book   9

Platoon column in support, Champagne, 1918   11

"Catch some alive _____"   14

The 2nd Engineers   18

A tortured area ... lit by flares and gun-flashes   21

The hill blazed into action—not all the rifle-fire had gone astray   24

Pencil sketches made on scraps of paper, in Belleau Wood   26

Combat patrol   29

A sprinkling of old-time Marines   32

Some of them had been this way before   35

Boche grenadier   37

So many chaps were not with the brigade very long   38

The Boche had out his pistol   40

Certain designated individuals watched   42

Men fought in its corpse-choked thickets   44

Bringing in German prisoners at St. Mihiel   46

Ration parties ... always sweated mightily and anticipated exciting incidents. . . .   47

"Bang away, Lulu—"   52

The automatic-rifle men   59

Prussians from Von Boehn's divisions in and around the Bois de Belleau   62

"Keep on to the left until you meet the Moroccans, and go forward...." 4.30 A. M., July 18, 1918   67

Listening-post rushed by Senegalese   70

A fighting swirl of Senegalese   73

List of Illustrations (continued)

Fighting from tree to tree in the woods south of
Soissons 76

With reason the Boche feared them worse than anything
living 79

The fighting in the woods at Soissons was close and
savage 82

A lieutenant of Marines and a German major, hand to
hand 85

Sketches made by Captain Thomason at Soissons on scraps
of paper taken from a feldwebel's note-book 88

Fighting north of Blanc Mont, Champagne 90

"Carry me back to Ole Virginny" 93

French grenadier—Blanc Mont 101

Those sawed-off shotguns they gave us at St. Mihiel 105

The shells began to drop into the trench 109

A flare during shelling in the front-line trenches 111

In the Essen trench—a runner 113

The morning of October 3rd came gray and misty—
a patrol 116

"Lordy, ain't we ever goin' to get outa this dam' place
an' get at 'em—?" 117

Others lay on the ground over which the battalion
passed 119

"Oh, Lordy! They've got us bracketed!" 121

Before zero hour 123

Flanking fire 126

The hush still hung around them as they moved out of the
flat and began to ascend the long gray slope ahead 127

List of Illustrations (continued)

The first shell came screaming down the line from
the right   129

"Here comes a battalion runner—what's up anyway?"   131

A few iron-souled Prussians—the Boche had such
men—stood up to meet bayonet with bayonet, and
died that way   134

The last few men are always the most difficult to kill   135

A machine-gunner, Champagne   137

"Mademoiselle from Armentières"   141

"Hey, yuh dog-robbin' battalion runner, you—
what's up!"   144

"He takes the war too serious"   146

The scout officer and the sergeant got him back some
way, both filled with admiration at his language   153

"War—sure—is—hell"   155

"Sweet Ad-o-line"   158

The cooks issued corn-bill hash and dared any man to
growl   161

A nice day for a hike   162

Men walked silent, remembering the old dead   165

One thick-bodied Boche. . . . His face in a cast of hate   168

They stood in stolid groups, wooden-faced   169

The 1st Battalion of the Rhine-5th Marines took the
road   170

Foreword

John W. Thomason, Jr. was an unlikely career Marine, and an even more improbable author and artist. Born on 18 February 1893 in the east Texas town of Huntsville, only the entry of America in the World War drew him away from his roots and into vocations of which his father disapproved. After high school, and short stints as an indifferent student at a variety of colleges, Thomason obtained employment as both a teacher and principal at a high school but his life remained unfulfilled. The U. S. declaration of war against Germany on 6 April 1917 changed his existence forever.

Thomason earned a commission as a second lieutenant in the Marine Corps Reserve on 6 August 1917, and was promoted to first lieutenant a month later as the smaller of the naval services began to expand rapidly in response to the war. Prior to the onset of hostilities, there were only 341 officers wearing forest green; by the end of the war, that number would reach over 2,400. In November, he reported to Quantico for pre-deployment training and embarked for France the following April. One of the officers in his replacement battalion, Laurence W. Stallings, would become an important literary figure after the war and play a significant part in the advancement of Thomason's own literary career. The eager Texan reported to the 49th Co.,

1st Battalion, 5th Marines, 4th Brigade (Marine), 2nd Division, American Expeditionary Forces as a platoon leader. For the rest of his time in France, Thomason sketched and jotted down notes whenever his demanding duties allowed.

In response to the German offensive that began in late May 1918, the 2nd Division, AEF deployed with another division to Château-Thierry to bolster the lines between the Marne and Paris. Thomason's brigade received orders to dig in along the Paris-Metz highway, just to the south of a largely unknown forest known locally as Belleau Wood, and halt the German advance. During the next two weeks, the Leathernecks counted more casualties than in any battle during their colorful history.

For two days, the *feld-grau* clad infantry attempted to breach the Marine lines but failed. On 6 June, the Marines moved into Belleau Wood to eject the Germans. Thomason and his men deployed across ripening wheat fields dotted with red poppies. During the assault, only he and his company commander, 1st Lt. George Hamilton, remained unscathed among the officers of the 49th Company. The Marine brigade counted more than a thousand dead and wounded, a casualty rate of over 50 percent.

During the subsequent deployment to Soissons in July, Thomason earned a Silver Star for personally leading a small force of Marines to wipe out a German machinegun nest. During the assault to retake the St. Mihiel salient in September 1918, the Marines found the enemy already in the process of evacuating the contested terrain. But at Blanc Mont the following month, Thomason's regiment suffered high casualties when the French division on its flank failed to keep pace during the advance. Murderous machinegun fire tore into the ranks of the 5th Marines; only 100 men survived out of Thomason's battalion.

Just as the 2nd Division, AEF, redeployed to join the Allies for the Meuse-Argonne offensive, Thomason came down with the dreaded influenza virus. After hospitalization, he rejoined the 5th Marines for occupation duty in Germany. With the return of the Marines from wartime duties in Europe in August 1919, Thomason applied for a regular commission; clearly by then, he had indicated a preference for soldiering over teaching or administrating at a high school in east Texas. When the Marine Corps trimmed its lineal list in response to post-war reductions, Thomason found himself listed as a captain, effective on 4 June 1920, but it meant deployment to the Caribbean. From November 1919 through October 1921, he commanded the mounted 37th Company at Camagüey, Cuba during the final days of the "Sugar Revolution." Thomason continued to write and sketch, but had yet to find a commercial outlet for his work.

During a subsequent tour at Marine Barracks, Naval Ammunition Depot, Dover, NJ, Thomason encountered Laurence T. Stallings, Jr. while on a visit to nearby Manhattan. His former comrade-in-arms from the 4th Brigade (Marine), AEF looked at Thomason's sketches and suggested a meeting with his publisher. The editors of Charles Scribner's Sons thought Thomason's work worthy of publication, and asked for text to accompany the art work. *Fix Bayonets and Other Stories* appeared in 1925; the most famous of Thomason's books.

Fix Bayonets and Other Stories is about the Old Corps, a Marine Corps that ended a year before Thomason joined it. The Naval Act of 1916 marked the division of the Old Corps and the New Corps. Prior to its passage, the Marine Corps counted only 300 officers and 9,000 enlisted men on its rolls. Everyone knew the officers or senior NCOs by name or reputation. Most enlisted men lived a rough-and-tumble life, with service records filled with numerous infractions of alcohol-related absences-without-leave (AWOL) and instances of venereal disease. Many of the old-time Marines traveled up and down the promotion ladder with alarming regularity, but accepted the punishments accompanying their transgressions as just an unwelcome aspect of their unique profession. Thomason served with many veterans of the Old Corps during his years as a

Marine, admired them unflinchingly, and lionized them through his sketches and writing.

Thomason spent the rest of his life alternating between stints ashore and at sea, a career pattern typical of the era. Instead of deploying with the Marines to Nicaragua in the late 1920s, the Major General Commandant loaned Thomason to the Army to assist in writing the history of the 2nd Division, AEF. By then, a worsening problem with alcoholism had begun to damage his health and professional reputation. Thomason's literary reputation had reached lofty heights mostly as a result of *Fix Bayonets and Other Stories*. Other books appeared during the interwar era, all under the imprint of Scribner's sons: *Red Pants and Other Stories* (1927); *Marines and Others* (1929); *Jeb Stuart* (1930); *Salt Winds and Gobi Dust* (1934); *The Adventures of Davy Crockett* (1934); *Adventures of General Marbot*; *Gone to Texas* (1937); *Lone Star Preacher* (1941); and, *-and a Few Marines* (1943).

Thomason attempted to balance his literary aspirations with a demanding military profession. After a tour with the Legation Guard in Peking, he was assigned as the aide-de-camp to Assistant Secretary of the Navy Henry L. Roosevelt. A Marine from the World War era, Col. Roosevelt took unusual pains to provide for the well-being of his subordinates; in Thomason's case, he managed to have the

Silver Star earned at Soissons upgraded to a Navy Cross. In 1937, Thomason graduated with distinction from the Army War College; a promotion to major followed quickly along with orders to attend the Naval War College. Despite the academic demands, Thomas continued to churn out books and even accepted H. L. Mencken's invitation to become chief editor of the *American Mercury.*

A two-year tour in the late 1930s at San Diego followed. Thomason commanded the Platoon Leader's Class, a form of officer candidate school offered to college students during the summer months. Then, he commanded the 2nd Battalion, 6th Marines. A lack of experience in tactical command of troops, prodigious efforts to propel his literary career forward, and continuing problems with alcoholism all combined to keep him out of a field assignment during World War Two. Instead Thomason became the chief of the Latin American Section, Office of Naval Intelligence. Then, he served in a minor position at fleet headquarters in Hawaii but his deteriorating health resulted in orders back to California. Thomason died at the naval hospital in San Diego on 12 March 1944.

The governor of Texas declared a statewide day of mourning, with flags flown at half-staff. The Navy christened a destroyer, the *John W. Thomason, Jr.* (DD760).

Thomason continues to be revered by readers of Leatherneck lore. Even before his untimely death, Thomason had deservedly earned the reputation as the "Kipling of the Old Corps."

Merrill L. Bartlett
Lieutenant Colonel, U. S. Marine Corps (Retired)

BATTLE SIGHT

IN THE fields near Marigny Marines of the 1st Battalion of the 5th found an amiable cow. There had been nothing in the way of rations that day; there were no prospects. All hands took thought and designated a robust Polish corporal as executioner. He claimed to have been a butcher in a former existence. He was leading the cow decently away from the road when a long gray car boomed up, halted with the touch of swank that Headquarters chauffeurs always affect, and disgorged a very angry colonel. The colonel's eye was cold upon the interested group around the cow. They stood now to attention, the cow alone remaining tranquil, with a poppy dangling from her languid mouth.

"Lieutenant, what are you doing there ——?"

"Sir, you see, the men haven't had anything to eat, and I thought, sir—we found this cow wanderin' around—we couldn't find any owner—we'd like to chip in and buy her—we were goin' to——"

"I see, sir, I see! You were going to kill this cow, the property of some worthy French family. You will bear in mind, lieutenant, that we are in France to protect the lives and property of our allies from the Germans—Release that animal at once! Your rations will be distributed as soon as possible—carry on——" The colonel departed, and four

3

or five 77s crashed into a little wood two hundred yards up the road. There were more shells in the same place. "Hi! Brother Boche must think there's a battery over there!"—"Well, there ain't—" The Marines sat down in the wheat and observed the cow.

"Property of our gallant allies—yeh!—" "Old man's in an awful humor—wonder what—" The lieutenant sucked a straw reflectively. His sergeant solaced himself with tobacco. The cow ruminated, quite content. She had nourished herself at will for three delightful days, since her people, in a farm over toward Torcy—where, at the minute, the Boche was killing off a battalion of French territorials—had incomprehensibly turned her out and vanished. Full-fed, she eyed the strangers without emotion.

"I was a quartermaster sergeant once, sir," said the platoon sergeant dreamily. "I remember just what the cuts of beef are. There'd be fine sirloin on that cow-critter, now. . . . Mr. Ashby (another flight of 77s burst in the wood), if we was to take that cow over an' tie her in that brush—she oughten to be out here in the open, anyway— might draw fire . . . shell's liable to hit anything, you know, sir——"

"Sergeant, you heard what the colonel said. But if you think she'd be safer—I'd suggest volunteers. And by the way, sergeant, I want a piece of tenderloin—the T-bone part——"

The cow was duly secured in the wood, men risking their lives thereby. The Boche shelled methodically for two hours, and the Marines were reduced to a fearful state of nerves—"Is that dam' heifer gonna live forever?—" Two or three kilometres away fighting was going on. The lieutenant, with his glass, picked up far, running figures on the slope of a hill. You caught a flicker, points of light on the gray-green fields—bayonets. Occasional wounded Frenchmen wandered back, weary, bearded men, very dirty. They looked with dull eyes at the Americans—

"Très mauvais, là-bas! Beaucoup Boche, là—" The Marines
were not especially interested. Their regiment had been a
year in France, training. Now they, too, were dirty and
tired and very hungry. The war would get along . . . it
always had.

Occasional wounded Frenchmen drifted back.

A week ago, Memorial Day, there had been no drills.
The 2d Division, up from a tour in the quiet Verdun
trenches, rested pleasantly around Bourmont. Rumors of
an attack by the 1st Division, at Cantigny, filtered in.

Cantigny was a town up toward Montdidier. Notions of geography were the vaguest—but it was in the north, where all the heavy fighting was. It appeared that the 2d was going up to relieve the 1st. . . . "Sure! we'll relieve 'em. But if they wanted a fight, why didn't they let us know in the first place?—We'd a-showed 'em what shock-troops can do!"

The division set out in camions; in the neighborhood of Meaux they were turned around and sent out the Paris-Metz road, along which the civilian population from the country between the Chemin des Dames and the Marne, together with the débris of a French army, was coming back. No man who saw that road those first days of June ever forgot it. A stream of old men and children and old and young women turned out of their homes between two sunrises, with what they could carry in their hands. You saw an ancient in a linen smock and sabots, trundling a wheelbarrow, whereon rode a woman as old as himself, with a feather-bed and a selection of copper pots and a string of garlic. There were families in amazing horse-drawn vehicles, models of the Third Empire, and horses about as old, clutching unreasonable selections of house-hold effects—onyx clocks and bird-cages and rabbits—what you like. Women carrying babies. Children—solemn little boys in black pinafores, and curly-headed, high-nosed little girls, trudging hand-in-hand. People of elegance and refinement on inadequate shoes. Broadfaced peasants. Inhabitants of a thousand peaceful little villages and farms, untouched by the war since 1914. Now the Boche was out again, and those quiet places, that had drowsed in obscurity while generations lived and worked and died, were presently to be known to all the world—names like Bouresches, and Belleau, and Fismes, and Vierzy, and Fismettes. They walked with their faces much on their shoulders, these people, and there was horror in their eyes.

The Marines took notice of another side of war. . . . "Hard on poor folks, war is." "You said it!"—"Say—think about my folks, an' your folks, out on the road like that! . . ." "Yeh. I'm thinkin' about it. An' when we meet that Boche, I'm gonna do something about it—Look—right nice-lookin' girl, yonder!"

There were French soldiers in the rout, too. Nearly all were wounded, or in the last stages of exhaustion. They did not appear to be first-line troops; they were old, bearded fellows of forty and forty-five, territorials; or mean, unpleasant-looking Algerians, such troops as are put in to hold a quiet sector. Seven or eight divisions of them had been in the line between Soissons and Rheims, which was, until 27 May, a quiet sector. On that day forty-odd divisions, a tidal wave of fighting Germans, with the greatest artillery concentration the Boche ever effected, was flung upon them, and they were swept away, as a levee goes before a flood. They had fought; they had come back, fighting, thirty-five miles in three days; and the Boche, though slowed up, was still advancing. They were holding him along the Marne, and at Château-Thierry a machine-gun battalion of the American 3d Division was piling up his dead in heaps around the bridge-heads, but to the northwest he was still coming. And to the northwest the 2d Division was gathering. During the 2d, the 3d, and the 4th of June it grouped itself, first the 4th Brigade of Marines, with some guns, and then the regular infantrymen of the 9th and 23d. Already, around Hautevesnes, there had been a brush with advancing Germans, and the Germans were given a new experience: rifle-fire that begins to kill at 800 yards; they found it very interesting. This was 5 June; the battalion near Marigny, on the left of the Marine Brigade, had a feeling that they were going in to-morrow. . . . The men thought lazily on events, and lounged in the wheat, and watched that clump of trees—

and at last an agonized bellow came on the echo of a
bursting shell— "Well—she's stopped one! Thought she
musta dug in— Let's go get it——"

Presently there was lots of steak, and later a bitter lesson
was repeated—mustn't build cooking-fires with green
wood, where the Boche can see the smoke. But everybody
lay down on full bellies. Before dark the last French were
falling back. Some time during the night Brigade sent
battle orders to the 1st Battalion of the 5th Marines, and
at dawn they were in a wood near Champillon. Nearly
every man had steaks in his mess-pan, and there was hope
for cooking them for breakfast. Instead . . .

Those were before the days of lavish maps, to which the
Americans afterwards attained. There was one map to
each company, exclusive property of the captain. Platoon
commanders had a look at it— "You're here. The objective
is a square patch of woods a kilometre and a half northeast,
about. See?—this. Form your platoons in four waves—the
guide will be right. Third Battalion is advancing their flank
to conform. French on the left. . . ." Platoons were formed
in four waves, the attack formation taught by the French,
a formation proved in trench warfare, where there was a
short way to go, and you calculated on losing the first
three waves and getting the fourth one to the objective.
The Marines never used it again. It was a formation un-
adapted for open warfare, and incredibly vulnerable. It
didn't take long to learn better, but there was a price to
pay for the learning.

The platoons came out of the woods as dawn was getting
gray. The light was strong when they advanced into the
open wheat, now all starred with dewy poppies, red as
blood. To the east the sun appeared, immensely red and
round, a handbreadth above the horizon; a German shell
burst black across the face of it, just to the left of the line.
Men turned their heads to see, and many there looked no
more upon the sun forever. "Boys, it's a fine, clear mornin'!

Sketches from Captain Thomason's note-book.

Guess we get chow after we get done molestin' these here Heinies, hey?"— One old non-com—was it Jerry Finnegan of the 49th?—had out a can of salmon, hoarded somehow against hard times. He haggled it open with his bayonet, and went forward so, eating chunks of goldfish from the point of that wicked knife. "Finnegan"—his platoon commander, a young gentleman inclined to peevishness before he'd had his morning coffee, was annoyed—"when you are quite through with your refreshments, you can—damn well fix that bayonet and get on with the war!" "Aye, aye, sir!" Finnegan was an old Haitian soldier, and had a breezy manner with very young lieutenants—"Th' lootenant want some?"—Two hours later Sergeant Jerry Finnegan lay dead across a Maxim gun with his bayonet in the body of the gunner. . . .

It was a beautiful deployment, lines all dressed and guiding true. Such matters were of deep concern to this outfit. The day was without a cloud, promising heat later, but now it was pleasant in the wheat, and the woods around looked blue and cool. Pretty country, those rolling wheatlands northwest of Château-Thierry, with copses of trees and little tidy forests where French sportsmen maintained hunting-lodges and game-preserves. Since the first Marne there had been no war here. The files found it very different from the mangled red terrain around Verdun, and much nicer to look at. "Those poppies, now. Right pretty, ain't they?"—a tall corporal picked one and stuck it in his helmet buckle, where it blazed against his leathery cheek. There was some shelling—not much, for few of the German guns had caught up, the French had lost all theirs, and the American artillery was still arriving.

Across this wheat-field there were more woods, and in the edge of these woods the old Boche, lots of him, infantry and machine-guns. Surely he had seen the platoons forming a few hundred yards away—it is possible that he did not believe his eyes. He let them come close before he opened

Platoon column in support, Champagne, 1918.
Drawn by Captain Thomason from notes made in front of Blanc Mont.

fire. The American fighting man has his failings. He is
prone to many regrettable errors. But the sagacious enemy
will never let him get close enough to see whom he is
attacking. When he has seen the enemy, the American
regular will come on in. To stop him you must kill him.
And when he is properly trained and has somebody to say
"Come on!" to him, he will stand as much killing as anybody on earth.

The platoons, assailed now by a fury of small-arms fire,
narrowed their eyes and inclined their bodies forward, like
men in heavy rain, and went on. Second waves reinforced
the first, fourth waves the third, as prescribed. Officers
yelled "Battlesight! fire at will"—and the leaders, making
out green-gray, clumsy uniforms and round pot-helmets in
the gloom of the woods, took it up with Springfields,
aimed shots. Automatic riflemen brought their chaut-
chauts into action from the hip—a chaut-chaut is as accu-
rate from the hip as it ever is—and wrangled furiously
with their ammunition-carriers— "Come on, kid—bag o'
clips!—" "Aw—I lent it to Ed to carry, last night—didn't
think—" "Yeh, and Ed lent it to a fence-post when he got
tired—get me some off a casualty, before I—" A very
respectable volume of fire came from the advancing platoons. There was yelling and swearing in the wheat, and
the lines, much thinned, got into the woods. Some grenades
went off; there was screaming and a tumult, and the "taka-
taka-taka-taka" of the Maxim guns died down. "Hi!
Sergeant!—hold on! Major said he wanted some prisoners—" "Well, sir, they looked like they was gonna start
somethin'—" "All right! All right! but you catch some
alive the next place, you hear?—" "Quickly, now—get
some kind of a line—" "Can't make four waves—" "Well,
make two—an' put the chaut-chauts in the second—no use
gettin' 'em bumped off before we can use 'em—" The
attack went on, platoons much smaller, sergeants and
corporals commanding many of them.

A spray of fugitive Boche went before the attack, holding where the ground offered cover, working his light machine-guns with devilish skill, retiring, on the whole, commendably. He had not expected to fight a defensive battle here, and was not heavily intrenched, but the place was stiff with his troops, and he was in good quality, as Marine casualty lists were presently to show. There was more wheat, and more woods, and obscure savage fighting among individuals in a brushy ravine. The attack, especially the inboard platoons of the 49th and 67th Companies, burst from the trees upon a gentle slope of wheat that mounted to a crest of orderly pines, black against the sky. A three-cornered coppice this side of the pines commanded the slope; now it blazed with machine-guns and rifles; the air was populous with wicked keening noises. Most of the front waves went down; all hands, very sensibly, flung themselves prone. "Can't walk up to these babies—" "No— won't be enough of us left to get on with the war—" "Pass the word: crawl forward, keepin' touch with the man on your right! Fire where you can—" That officer, a big man, who had picked up a German light machine-gun somewhere, with a vague idea of using it in a pinch, or, in any case, keeping it for a souvenir, received the attention of a heavy Maxim and went down with a dozen bullets through his chest.

Men crawled forward; the wheat was agitated, and the Boche, directing his fire by observers in tree-tops, browned the slope industriously. Men were wounded, wounded again as the lines of fire swept back and forth, and finally killed. It helped some to bag the feldwebels in the trees; there were men in that line who could hit at 750 yards, three times out of five. Sweating, hot, and angry with a bleak, cold anger, the Marines worked forward. They were there, and the Germans, and there was nothing else in the clanging world. An officer, risking his head above the wheat, observed progress, and detached a corporal with his squad

"Catch some alive——"

to get forward by the flank. "Get far enough past that flank gun, now, close as you can, and rush it—we'll keep it busy.". . . Nothing sounds as mad as rifle-fire, staccato, furious— The corporal judged that he was far enough, and raised with a yell, his squad leaping with him. He was not past the flank; two guns swung that way, and cut the squad down like a grass-hook levels a clump of weeds. . . . They lay there for days, eight Marines in a dozen yards, face down on their rifles. But they had done their job. The men in the wheat were close enough to use the split-second interval in the firing. They got in, cursing and stabbing. Meanwhile, to the left a little group of men lay in the wheat under the very muzzle of a gun that clipped the stalks around their ears and riddled their combat packs —firing high by a matter of inches and the mercy of God. A man can stand just so much of that. Life presently ceases to be desirable; the only desirable thing is to kill that gunner, kill him with your hands! One of them, a corporal named Geer, said: "By God, let's get him!" And they got him. One fellow seized the spitting muzzle and up-ended it on the gunner; he lost a hand in the matter. Bayonets flashed in, and a rifle-butt rose and fell. The battle tore through the coppice. The machine-gunners were brave men, and many of the Prussian infantry were brave men, and they died. A few streamed back through the brush, and hunters and hunted burst in a frantic medley on the open at the crest of the hill. Impartial machine-guns, down the hill to the left, took toll of both. Presently the remnants of the assault companies were panting in the trees on the edge of the hill. It was the objective of the attack, but distance had ceased to have any meaning, time was not, and the country was full of square patches of woods. In the valley below were more Germans, and on the next hill. Most of the officers were down, and all hands went on.

They went down the brushy slope, across a little run, across a road where two heavy Maxims were caught sitting, and mopped up and up the next long, smooth slope. Some Marines branched off down that road and went into the town of Torcy. There was fighting in Torcy, and a French avion reported Americans in it, but they never came out again . . . a handful of impudent fellows against a battalion of Sturm-truppen. . . . Then the men who mounted the slope found themselves in a cleared area, full of orderly French wood-piles, and apparently there was a machine-gun to every wood-pile. Jerry Finnegan died here, sprawled across one of them. Lieutenant Somers died here. One lieutenant found himself behind a wood-pile, with a big auto-rifleman. Just across from them, very near, a machine-gun behind another wood-pile was searching for them. The lieutenant, all his world narrowed to that little place, peered vainly for a loophole; the sticks were jumping and shaking as the Maxim flailed them; bullets rang under his helmet. "Here, Morgan," he said, "I'll poke my tin hat around this side, and you watch and see if you can get the chaut-chaut on them—" He stuck the helmet on his bayonet, and thrust it out. Something struck it violently from the point, and the rifle made his fingers tingle. The chaut-chaut went off, once. In the same breath there was an odd noise above him . . . the machine-gun . . . he looked up. Morgan's body was slumping down to its knees; it leaned forward against the wood, the chaut-chaut, still grasped in a clenched hand, coming to the ground butt first. The man's head was gone from the eyes up; his helmet slid stickily back over his combat pack and lay on the ground. . . . "My mother," reflected the lieutenant, "will never find my grave in this place!" He picked up the chaut-chaut, and examined it professionally, noting a spatter of little thick red drops on the breech, and the fact that the clip showed one round expended. The charging handle was back. He got to his feet with deliberation, laid the gun across the wood-pile, and sighted . . . three Boche with very red faces; their eyes looked pale under their deep helmets. . . . He gave them the whole clip, and they appeared to wilt. Then he came away from there. Later he was in the little run at the foot of the hill with three men, all wounded. He never knew how he got there. It just happened.

Later in the day the lieutenant was back on the pine-crested hill, now identified as Hill 142. Captain Hamilton was there, one or two other officers, and a handful of the 49th and 67th Companies; a semblance of a line was organized. "Nothing on the right or left; all right, we'll just stay here—" Some people from the 8th Company had a Hotchkiss gun, and some Boche Maxims were put in position. It was said that Blake, of the 17th, had been up, and was bringing the company in. The Boche indulged himself in violent shelling and raked the hill savagely with all the machine-guns in the world. From the direction of Torcy a counter-attack developed; the Boche was filtering cleverly forward and forming somewhere on the Torcy road, in cover. The Marines were prone, slings adjusted, killing him. "It's a quarter-point right windage—" "Naw! not a breath of air! Use zero—" A file of sweating soldiers, burdened with picks and shovels in addition to bandoleers and combat gear, came trotting from the right. A second lieutenant, a reddish, rough-looking youngster, clumped up and saluted. "You in charge here?" he said to the Marine officer. "I'm Lieutenant Wythe of the 2d Engineers, with a detachment. I'm to report to you for orders." "Well— captain's right up yonder—how many men you got?" "Twenty-two, sir" "Fine! That makes thirty-six of us, includin' me—just flop right here, and we'll hold this line. Orders are to dig in here—but that can wait—see yonder——?"

Those Engineers, their packs went one way and their tools another, and they cast themselves down happily. "What range, buddy?—usin' any windage—?" A hairy

The 2d Engineers.

non-com got into his sling and laid out a little pile of clips.
. . . There was always good feeling between the Marines of
the 2d Division and the Regular Army units that formed
it, but the Marines and the 2d Engineers—"Say, if I ever
got a drink, a 2d Engineer can have half of it!—Boy, they
dig trenches and mend roads all night, and they fight all
day! An' when us guys get all killed off, they just come up
an' take over the war! They's no better folks anywhere
than the Engineers. . . ."

The Boche wanted Hill 142; he came, and the rifles broke
him, and he came again. All his batteries were in action, and
always his machine-guns scourged the place, but he could
not make head against the rifles. Guns he could understand;
he knew all about bombs and auto-rifles and machine-guns
and trench-mortars, but aimed, sustained rifle-fire, that
comes from nowhere in particular and picks off men—it
brought the war home to the individual and demoralized
him.

And trained Americans fight best with rifles. Men get
tired of carrying grenades and chaut-chaut clips; the guns
cannot, even under most favorable conditions, keep pace
with the advancing infantry. Machine-gun crews have a
way of getting killed at the start; trench-mortars and one-
pounders are not always possible. But the rifle and bayonet
goes anywhere a man can go, and the rifle and the bayonet
win battles. Toward midday, this 6th of June, 1918, the
condition around Hill 142 stabilized. A small action,
fought by battalions over a limited area of no special
importance, it gave the Boche something new to think
about, and it may be that people who write histories will
date an era from it.

Between attacks the stretcher-bearers and the Red Cross
men on both sides did their utmost for the wounded who
were scattered through the wheat around the hill, and who
now, under the torture of stiffening wounds and the hot
sun, began to cry out. As the afternoon advanced, you

heard pitiful voices! little and thin across the fields: *"Ach, Himmel, hilf, hilf! Brandighe! . . . Liebe Gott, brandighe!"* . . . "First-aid—this way, First-aid, for the love of God!" . . . From most wounds men do not appear to suffer greatly at first. There is the hot impulse of the attack, and perhaps a certain shock from the missile, so that the nerves are numb. One has gone forward with the tide at the highest; life is a light thing to lay down, death a light thing to venture; yonder is the enemy; one has come a long way to meet him, and now the affair can be taken up personally. Then something hits—the wheat cuts off all the world. An infernal racket goes on somewhere—Springfields and Mausers, Maxim guns and Hotchkiss—sometimes closer, sometimes receding. Bullets zip and drone around. There may be shells, shrapnel, and H. E., searching the ground, one can hear them coming. "Is it gonna hit me—is it gonna hit me, O Lawd— Christ! that was close!" Presently pain, in recurring waves. Pride may lock a man's lips awhile . . . left long enough, most men break, and no blame to them. A hundred brave dead, lying where the guns cut them down, are not so pitiful as one poor wailing fellow in a dressing-station. . . .

Forward of the hill, German stretcher-bearers moved openly, unmolested, at first. The Marines watched them curiously. The enemy, his works are always interesting. A sergeant said: "Hi! Look at those Fritzies yonder, right off the road, there—" A lieutenant got his glass on them; two big men, one with a yellow beard, wearing Red Cross brassards. They carried a loaded stretcher; it looked like a man lying with his knees drawn up, under a blanket. "Humph! Got him well covered—officer, probably." One stumbled, or the wind blew, and an end of the blanket flapped back, disclosing unmistakably the blunt snout of a heavy Maxim.— "So that's it, eh? Slover—Jennings— Heald—got a rifle, Cannon? Range 350—let 'em have it— we can play that game, too—" Thereafter it was hard on

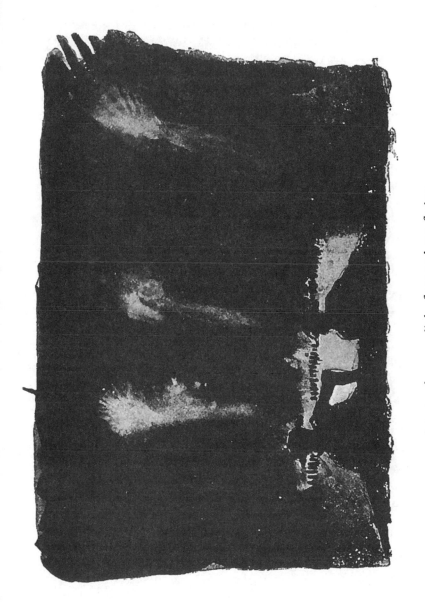

A tortured area . . . lit by flares and gun-flashes.

Red Cross men and wounded; hard, in fact, on everybody.
Like reasonable people, the Americans were willing to learn
from the Boche, from anybody who could teach them; and
if the Boche played the game that way—they could meet
him at it. "Schrechlichkeit—if he wants frightfulness, we
can give it to him—" Later there was a letter, taken from
a dead feldwebel in the Bois de Belleau— "The Americans
are savages. They kill everything that moves. . . ."

Late in the afternoon a great uproar arose to the right.
There was more artillery up now, more machine-guns,
more of everything. The 3d Battalion of the 6th Marines
and the 3d Battalion of the 5th attacked the town called
Bouresches and the wood known as Bois de Belleau. They
attacked across the open, losing hideously. Platoons were
shot down entire. The colonel commanding the 6th Regiment, farther forward than regimental commanders have
any business being, was shot and evacuated. Lieutenant
Robertson got into Bouresches, with twenty men out of
some hundred who started, threw the Boche out, and held
it. They gained a footing in the rocky ledges at the edge
of the Bois de Belleau, suffering much from what was be-
lieved to be a machine-gun nest at this point. They tried
to leave it and go on, with a containing force to watch it;
they found that the whole wood was a machine-gun nest.

Night descended over a tortured area of wheat and
woodland, lit by flares and gun-flashes, flailed by machine-
guns, and in too many places pitiful with crying of
wounded who had lain all the day untended in a merciless
sun. Stretcher-bearers and combat patrols roamed over it
in the dark. Water parties and ration parties groped back
from forward positions over unknown trails. There were
dog-fights all over the place, wild alarms, and hysterical
outbreaks of rifle-fire. It was the same with the Boche;
he knew the ground better, and he was determined to
repossess it. His people filtered back through the American

strong points, for the Marines did not hold a continuous line; isolated positions were connected by patrols and machine-guns laid for interlocking fire.

At the southern angle of Hill 142 the 49th Company put out a listening-post—one man down the slope a little way, to watch for visitors. In the night there was a trampling, a grunt, and one scream—"Boche!"— At once the hill blazed into action—weary men overspent, they fired into the dark until their pieces were hot. And after they found the listening-post fellow, bayoneted. And down the hill a little huddle of new dead. Not all the rifle-fire had gone astray.

Back in Brigade, officers bent over maps and framed orders for a stronger attack on the Bois de Belleau at dawn. . . . Brigade was writing also to Division: ". . . . casualties severe . . . figures on which to base call for replacements will be submitted as soon as possible. . . ."

II

REPLACEMENTS

At the crossroads beyond La Voie du Chatelle they met the War.

Behind them, crammed somehow into weeks, were Quantico, the transport, Brest, a French troop-train. Then there was the golden country around St. Aignan, the "Saint Onion" of Americans, a country full of growing wheat and fields of red-topped clover, picture-book houses, and neat little forests. A country stripped of men, where the women were competent and kindly. Almost any place you could get noble omelets and white wine that tasted better than chlorinated water—good kick in it, too. "I tell you, Boots, an' you remember it, this here France is a fine place to have a war in. Now, Haiti, an' in Nicaragua, an' in China, it's nowhere near as good. I hope Germany will be as good, when—" So Sergeant McGee, with his double rows

The hill blazed into action—not all the rifle-fire had gone astray.

of ribbons and his hash marks, over a canteen full of *eau de vie*—old-timer he was.

The war was represented by demoniac non-coms, instructors in this and that. Bayonet drills— "Come on, now; lemme hear you *'What do we wash our bay'nets in?— German blood!'*— Aw— sing out like you meant it, you dam' replacements! I'll swear, it's a shame to feed animals like you to the Germans—" Gas-mask drill— "Take more than five seconds, an' your Maw gets a Gold Star— Now!— the gas-alert position— O, for Gawd's sake, you guy, you wit' the two left feet—" "But, sergeant, I find that I have a certain difficulty—" Sergeants also swear terribly. . . . There was every kind of drill, eight hours a day of it, and police work.

Rumors of great battles in the north. Glum and sad civilians—they were glum and sad everywhere in France, that spring of 1918—talking in anxious groups after the town crier with his drum passed. Another troop-train— maybe the same train that was carelessly left alongside a train containing the wine ration for some French division, the papers in which case are probably still accumulating. Camions after that. The replacements debussed late of a June afternoon and went up a great white road between exactly spaced poplars. They marched first in column of squads, then in column of files, platoons on opposite sides of the empty road. At the crest of a slope the column stopped. You could see, hanging above the sky-line to the north and east, curious shapes— "Look like a elephant's head, bows on, wit' his ears out, don't they, sergeant?" The tall non-com who was guiding the column—a silent man—observed to the replacement officer in charge: "We'll stop here, sir. Boche sausages yonder—observation balloons —see the whole country. We'll wait till dark."

The detachment was glad to fall out, off the road. It sat in little groups, silent for the most part, and listened to a mutter and a rumble in the direction of the blimps. A

Pencil sketches made on scraps of paper, in Belleau Wood.

dark, high plane came into view from the east; its motor
filled the ear with a deep, vibrant droning, oddly ominous.
All at once the air around it was stippled with little puff-
balls, white against the blue. You could hear the drumming
of artillery, and the faint cough of bursting shrapnel, very
far off. The plane went away. "—Yes, sir. Anti-aircraft
stuff. Pretty, but it seldom hits anything—though it does
run 'em off. Theirs is black. . . ." The sergeant only spoke
when spoken to; there was a look about his eyes—he was
the survivor of a platoon that was sixty strong two days
before. The sun set, and the day drowsed into the long twilight. Presently the sergeant said: "We can move now, sir."
The replacements moved, making no conversation.

A little country road led them off the highway. They
passed a shattered farmhouse where a few soldiers lounged
in the dusk. "Regimental, sir. Gets shelled a lot. No, sir,
they don't expect you to report. Somebody on the road to
meet you. . . ." A little group of officers rose out of the
ditch, yawning. They looked slack and tired. "Replacement column? You in charge? Yes—assignments made
back in Brigade. You'll go to— Henry: your battalion gets
a hundred and seventy, with five officers. Take 'em off the
head of the column—tell Major Turrill——"

The detachment followed the officer called Henry, who
set what they considered an immoderate pace. He passed
the word: "Don't bunch up; if a plane comes over low,
don't look up at it—he can see your faces; no smokin', an'
don't talk—" Sergeant McGee thought audibly: "Where
have I seen that bird? Was it in Managua, that time they
broke me for . . . was it in Cuba?—where the devil—he was
somebody's sergeant-major—" They turned off the lane
and went through a wheatfield. The sky was sword-blade
blue, with a handful of stars. There was a loom of woods
ahead, the tops of them outlined by greenish flares ceaselessly ascending somewhere beyond. They heard a machine-
gun. "Sounds like one of these here steam-riveters, now,

don't it? . . ." A vagrant puff of wind blew a smell across
the column, a smell terrible and searing to the nose. "Phew!
dead hawses—" The officer named Henry spoke crisply.
"Those are not," he said, "dead horses." The replacements
sweated and felt cold, and thirsty too. They went on,
very silent.

They went through a gap in a hedge and were at another
crossroads. "Fall out here, an' form combat packs. Leave
your stuff under the hedge. Take one blanket. Come on—
quickly, now!—an' don't bunch up!—" The replacements
formed combat packs expertly, remembering Parris Island
and Quantico. "Smartly, now! Come by here, fill your
pockets—each man take two boxes hard bread— Where'll
you carry them? How in hell do I know— There!"

Two goods-boxes sat close together, and the men filed
between them. One box had dried prunes in it, the other
bread. "Don't stop! don't stop! Right down that road, an'
keep movin'!"

Out over the woods a sound started, a new sound. It
was a rumbling whine, it grew to a roar, and a 77 crashed
down just beyond the crossroads. A cloud blacker than the
night leaped up, shot with red fire— "Lie down, all hands!"
Another landed at once; the air was full of singing parti-
cles. The men, flat on their faces, in the dark, waited
numbly for the next order. There were a dozen or so shells
all around the place. The last one hit between the two
goods-boxes, where a man was lying. The boxes and the
man vanished in a ruddy cloud—better than if he'd gotten
it in the belly and rolled around screaming. . . . There were
no more shells— "Say, you know, I saw a arm an' a rifle
goin' up wit' that burst—I—who was he, anyway?—"
"Keep quiet, there! All right! on your feet—right down
that road—" the officer ordered, and added to himself—
"Dam' it! Should have remembered they shell La Voie du
Chatelle every night this time—but they acted fine. . . ."
A voice spoke up, excited, amused: "Say! Sergeant McGee

Combat patrol.

—anything like that in Vera Cruz?" "Pipe down, you Boot."

They went down a wood-road, black as a pocket, the files pressing close to keep the man ahead in sight. They went lightly, a weight off each man's mind. They had been shelled, and nobody had run away, and only one man hurt! Most men are afraid when they go up to the front; and what they fear most is the fear of seeming afraid. . . . They were ordered to fix bayonets. The road began to have inequalities in it. There were noises, explosions, around in the dark. The machine-guns sounded nearer; the flares showed more starkly on the sky. A man fell into a hole, and there was an acrid smell that caught at your windpipe. Just ahead, down the road, came a bright flash and a roar, and fragments ripped through the woods, and they heard a lamentable crying, getting weaker: "First aid! first aid—" The column came to a dead mule and the wreck of a cart lying athwart the road, and a smoking hole, and a smell of high explosive, and the sharp reek of blood. There was a struggling group, somebody working swiftly in the dark, a whiteness of bandages, and the white blur of a man's torso. "Lie still, damn you!"— "O, Jesus! Jesus Christ! Jesus Christ!—Ahhhhh! Go easy, you—" "Hell, I know it hurts, guy, but I got to get this bandage on, haven't I? Come on—quit kickin'—" Passing around the mule, a man stepped on something neither hard nor soft—nothing else on earth feels that way—and he floundered to one side, cursing hysterically.— "Quiet, back there—pass the word, no talking!" The files obediently passed the word. The column groped on in the dark.

It came out of the woods into a pale stone town— Champillon. There were no lights in the houses; the place had an air of death about it. There was a well by Champillon, where the water-parties came back from the lines in the night for water. . . . One canteenful was a man's allowance for each twenty-four hours. Men, after a time, made a shift to wash and shave and live not too thirsty out of one canteen a day. The replacements met two spectres who bore between them, on a long stick, twenty-odd canteens—the canteens of a platoon. "Hey! Guy!—" this in a hoarse whisper—"you comin' up to relieve us?" "Hell, no!" a guide answered. "These is 1st Battalion replacements." "I'll be goddam'. Gonna leave us in forever— Ain't we ever gonna be relieved?—" "Close up, there, and silence——"

There was a Ph.D. from Harvard in that sweating file, a big, pale, unhandy private, hounded habitually by sergeants, and troubled with indigestion and patriotism. For all his training, a pack was not at home on his shoulders or a rifle easy in his hands. He was aware of his panoply of war—the full belt dragging at his loins, the straps that cut into his shoulders, the bulge of prunes in his blouse-pockets, and his Springfield, increasingly heavy. He reflected, feeling for the road with clumsy hob-nails—for he was blind in the dark— "Now, those men are undoubtedly of the professional-soldier type. It is all a business with them. They are tired and they want to rest, and they say so frankly. No matter how tired I was, I'd never have the courage to say I wanted a relief. I'd want to awfully, but——"

He thought of the pleasant study back Cambridge way, of the gold-and-blue sergeant under the "First to Fight!" recruiting poster—"Your job, too, fella! Come on an' help lick the Hun! You don't wanta wait to be drafted, a big guy like you! We can use you in the Marines—" A hearty, red-necked ruffian—extremely competent in his vocation, no doubt. Good enough chaps. Yes . . . but . . . tea by a sea-coal fire in the New England twilight, and clever talk of art and philosophic anarchism—one wrote fastidious essays on such things for the more discriminating reviews—scholarly abstractions. . . . Of all the stupid, ignorant, uncivilized things, a war! Who coined that phrase, civilized war-

A sprinkling of old-time Marines.

fare? There was no such thing! . . . Here, in the most civilized country on earth. . . . The neighborhood of Château-Thierry . . . Montaigne's town, wasn't it? The kings of France had a château near it, once. And yet it was always a cockpit . . . since AEtius rolled back Attila in the battle of the nations, at Châlons—Napoleon fought Champ-Aubert and Montmirail around here—always war—

The column was through Champillon, dipping into a black hollow. More shell-holes in the road here. . . . All at once there was a new shell-hole, and the doctor of philosophy, sometime private of Marines, lay beside it, very neatly beheaded, with the rifle, that had been such a bore to keep clean, across his knees, and dried prunes spilling out of the pockets that he never had learned to button. The column went on. At dawn a naval medico attached to the Marine Brigade, with a staff officer, passed that way.

"Odd, the wounds you see," observed the naval man, professionally interested. He looked curiously. "I couldn't have done a neater decapitation than that myself. Wonder who—took his identification tags with it. I see. Replacement, by his uniform—" (For the 5th and 6th Regiments had long since worn out their forester-green Marine uniforms, and were wearing army khaki, while the replacements came in new green clothing.) The staff officer picked up the rifle, snapped back the bolt, and squinted expertly down the bore. "Disgustin'," he said. "Sure he was a replacement. You never catch an old-timer with a bore like that—filthy! Bet there hasn't been a rag through it in a week. You know, surgeon, I was looking at some of the rifles of that bunch of machine-gunners lying in the brush just across from Battalion; they were beautiful. Never saw better kept pieces. Fine soldiers in a lot of ways, these Boche! . . ."

Meantime the column had passed into heavier woods, and halted where the rifles ahead sounded very near. They saw dugouts, betrayed by the thread of candle-light around the edges of the blankets that cloaked their entrances. One was a dressing-station, by the sound and the smell of it. The officer named Henry ducked into the other. There a stocky major sat up on the floor and rolled a cigarette, which he lighted at a guttering candle. "Replacements in? Well, what do they look like?—"

"Same men I saw in the training area last month, sir. A sprinkling of old-time Marines—Sergeant McGee, that we broke for something or other in Panama, is with 'em— and the rest of them are young college lads and boys off the farm—fine material, sir. Not much drill, but they probably know how to shoot, they take orders, and they don't scare worth a cent! Shelled coming in, at Voie du Chatelle, and some more this side of Champillon—several casualties. No confusion—nothing like a panic—laid down and waited for orders—did exactly as they were told—fine men, sir!"

"All right! All right! Rush 'em right up to the companies. Guides are waiting around outside—company commanders have their orders about distribution. Start with the 49th and drop 'em off as you go along. They'll do— they'll have to! . . ."

III

THE BOIS DE BELLEAU

They tried new tactics to get the bayonets into the Bois de Belleau. Platoons—very lean platoons now—formed in small combat groups, deployed in the wheat, and set out toward the gloomy wood. Fifty batteries were working on it, all the field pieces of the 2nd Division, and what the French would lend. The shells ripped overhead, and the wood was full of leaping flame, and the smoke of H. E. and shrapnel. The fire from its edge died down. It was late in the afternoon; the sun was low enough to shine under the edge of your helmet. The men went forward at a walk, their shoulders hunched over, their bodies inclined, their eyes on the edge of the wood, where shrapnel was raising a hell of a dust. Some of them had been this way before; their faces were set bleakly. Others were replacements, a

Some of them had been this way before.

month or so from Quantico; they were terribly anxious to do the right thing, and they watched zealously the sergeants and the corporals and the lieutenants who led the way with canes.

One such group, over to the left, followed a big young officer, a replacement, too, but a man who had spent a week

in Bouresches and was to be considered a veteran, as such
things went in those days, when so many chaps were not
with the brigade very long. He had not liked Bouresches,
which he entered at night, and where he lived obscenely in
cellars with the dead, and saw men die in the orange flash
of minenwerfer shells, terribly and without the consola-
tion of glory. Here, at last, was attack. . . . He thought,
absently watching his flank to see that it guided true—
guide centre was the word—of the old men who had
brought him up to tales of Lee's Army of Northern Vir-
ginia, in the War of the Southern Confederacy. Great battles, glamorous attacks, full of the color and the high-
hearted élan of chivalry. Jackson at Chancellorsville; Pick-
ett at Gettysburg—that was a charge for you—the red
Southern battle-flags, leading like fierce brightwinged birds
the locked ranks of fifteen gray brigades, and the screech-
ing Rebel yell, and the field-music, fife and drum, rattling
out "The Girl I Left Behind Me":

> "Oh, if ever I get through this war,
>   And the Lincoln boys don't find me,
> I'm goin' to go right back again
>   To the girl I left behind me—"

No music here, no flags, no bright swords, no lines of
battle charging with a yell. Combat groups of weary men,
in drab and dirty uniforms, dressed approximately on a
line, spaced "so that one shrapnel-burst cannot include
more than one group," laden like mules with gas-masks,
bandoleers, grenades, chaut-chaut clips, trudging forward
without haste and without excitement, they moved on an
untidy wood where shells were breaking, a wood that did
not answer back, or show an enemy. In its silence and
anonymity it was far more sinister than any flag-crowned
rampart, or stone walls topped with crashing volleys from
honest old black-powder muskets—he considered these

Boche grenadier.

things and noted that the wood was very near, and that the
German shells were passing high and breaking in the rear,

So many chaps were not with the brigade very long.

where the support companies were waiting. His own artillery appeared to have lifted its range; you heard the shells
farther in, in the depths of the wood.

The air snapped and crackled all around. The sergeant
beside the lieutenant stopped, looked at him with a frozen,
foolish smile, and crumpled into a heap of old clothes.

Something took the kneecap off the lieutenant's right knee
and his leg buckled under him. He noticed, as he fell sideways, that all his men were tumbling over like duck-pins;
there was one fellow that spun around twice, and went
over backward with his arms up. Then the wheat shut him
in, and he heard cries and a moaning. He observed curiously
that he was making some of the noise himself. How could
anything hurt so? He sat up to look at his knee—it was
bleeding like the deuce!—and as he felt for his first-aid
packet, a bullet seared his shoulder, knocking him on his
back again. For a while he lay quiet and listened to odd,
thrashing noises around him, and off to the left a man began
to call, very pitifully. At once he heard more machine-gun
fire—he hadn't seemed to hear it before—and now the bullets were striking the ground and ricocheting with peculiar
whines in every direction. One ripped into the dirt by his
cheek and filled his eyes and his mouth with dust. The
lamentable crying stopped; most of the crawling, thrashing noises stopped. He himself was hit again and again, up
and down his legs, and he lay very still.

Where he lay he could just see a tree-top—he was that
near the wood. A few leaves clung to it; he tried to calcu-
late, from the light on them, how low the sun was, and how
long it would be until dark. Stretcher-bearers would be
along at dark, surely. He heard voices, so close that he could
distinguish words:

"*Caput?*"

"*Nein—nicht alles—*"

Later, forgetting those voices, he tried to wriggle backward into a shell-hole that he remembered pasing. He was
hit again, but somehow he got into a little shell-hole, or got
his body into it, head first. He reflected that he had bled so
much that a head-downward position wouldn't matter,
and he didn't want to be hit again. Men all dead, he supposed. He couldn't hear any of them. He seemed to pass
out, and then to have dreamy periods of consciousness. In

The Boche had out his pistol.

one of these periods he saw the sky over him was dark, metallic blue; it would be nearly night. He heard somebody coming on heavy feet, and cunningly shut his eyes to a slit . . . playing dead. . . . A German officer, a stiff, immaculate fellow, stood over him, looking at him. He lay very still, trying not to breathe. The Boche had out his pistol, a short-barrelled Luger, rested it on his left forearm, and fired deliberately. He felt the bullet range upward through the sole of his foot, and something excruciating happened in his ankle. Then one called, and the German passed from his field of vision, returning his pistol as he went. . . .

Later, trying to piece things together, he was in an ambulance, being jolted most infernally. And later he asked a nurse by his bed: "I say, nurse, tell me—did we get the Bois de Belleau?"—"Why, last June!" she said. "It's time you were coming out of it! This is August. . . ."

IV

COMING OUT

The battalion lay in unclean holes on the far face of Bois de Belleau, which was "now U. S. Marine Corps entirely." The sun was low over Torcy, and all the battalion, except certain designated individuals, slept. The artillery, Boche and American, was engaged in counter-battery work, and the persecuted infantry enjoyed repose. The senior lieutenant of the 49th Company, bedded down under a big rock with his orderly, came up from infinite depths of slumber with his pistol out, all in one swift motion. You awoke like that in the Bois de Belleau. . . . Jennings, company runner, showed two buck-teeth at him and said: "Sir, the cap'n wants to see you——"

They crawled delicately away from the edge of the wood, to a trail that took you back under cover, and found the captain frying potatoes in bacon grease. "Going out to-night, by platoons. Start as soon as it's dark, with the

17th. We are next. 6th Regiment outfit makin' the relief—
96th Company for us. They've been here before, so you
needn't leave anybody to show them the ground. Soon as
they get to you, beat it. Got a sketch of the map? Have

Certain designated individuals watched.

your platoon at Bois Gros-Jean—you know, beyond Brigade, on the big road—at daylight. Battalion has chow
there.—Got it?—Good——"

The lieutenant went happily back to his men. The word
had already gotten around, by the grape-vine route, and
grinning heads stuck out of every hole. "Well, sergeant,
pass the word to get set—goin' out to-night—" "Yes, sir!

Ready right now! Is the division bein' relieved?"—"No,
6th Regiment comin' in—" "Well, sir, I hope to God they
ain't late. Did you hear, sir, anything about us goin' back
to St. Denis, and gettin' liberty in Paris, an' a month's rest
—" That unaccountable delusion persisted in the Marine
Brigade through all of June and into July. It never happened. "No, I didn't hear any such thing. But it's enough
to get out of here. This place is like the wrath of God!"

It was. To begin with, it had been a tangled, rocky wood
of a few kilometres, the shooting-preserve of a French family in happier days. Even now you could see where a sort
of hunting-lodge had been; they said some Marines had
crawled in and bombed a Boche headquarters out of it. The
first of June it was rather a pretty place, with great trees
and flowery underbrush, all green and new in the full tide
of spring. It was a place of no particular military importance other than local. But the chance of war made it a
symbol. The German rolled down to it like a flood, driving
before him forlorn fragments of wrecked French divisions,
all the way from the Chemin des Dames. It was the spear-
head of his last great thrust on Paris. The Americans of the
2nd Division were new troops, untried in this war, regarded
with uneasy hopefulness by the Allies. Their successes came
when the Allies very greatly needed a success; for not since
1914 had the Boche appeared so terrible as in this, the
spring of 1918. For a space the world watched the Bois de
Belleau uneasily, and then with pride and an awakened
hope. Men saw in it, foreshadowed, Soissons, and the 8th
of August, that Ludendorf was to call "the black day of
the war," and an event in a car on a railroad siding, in the
misty November forest of Senlis.

But the men who fought here saw none of these things.
Good German troops, with every device of engineering
skill, and all their cunning gained in war, poured into the
wood. Battalions of Marines threw themselves against it.
Day and night for nearly a month men fought in its

corpse-choked thickets, killing with bayonet and bomb and machine-gun. It was gassed and shelled and shot into the semblance of nothing earthly. The great trees were all down; the leaves were blasted off, or hung sere and black-

Men fought in its corpse-choked thickets. . . .

ened. It was pockmarked with shell craters and shallow dugouts and hasty trenches. It was strewn with all the débris of war, Mauser rifles and Springfields, helmets, German and American, unexploded grenades, letters, knapsacks, packs, blankets, boots; a year later, it is said, they were still finding unburied dead in the depths of it. Finally it was taken, by inches.

Now the battalion turned its backs to the tangle and watched with languid interest the shrapnel that one of the batteries of our 15th Field was showering on the ruined airdrome in front of Torcy. The white puffballs were tinged pink by the setting sun, and jets of reddish dust went up from the ground under the bursts. A Boche battery was replying, and heavy shells rumbled far above, searching transport lines. Those nights, up in northern France, came late and went early. A man could sit on the edge of his hole, prairie-dog fashion, and write a letter at 10:30; it was not safe to move in the open until after 11:00; it was nearly midnight when the relieving troops came in. The lieutenant's opposite number reported, chap he hadn't seen since Quantico, back in another lifetime—"Well, here we are! Out you go—" "I say, is it you, Bob? Heard you were killed—" "Oh, not at all—heard the same thing about you —not strange; lot of serious accidents have happened around here—" "Well, good luck—" "Sure—bon chance, eh?—so-long———"

The platoon left the wood and angled down to the Torcy road. A string of shells howled overhead, 88s by the sound of them, and broke on the road. The lieutenant halted and watched: "Dam' unusual, shellin' here this time of night— must know it's a relief—" It was the conviction of all that the Boche knew everything, down to the movements of the lowest corporal.—"I think we'll cut a corner, and take a chance of gettin' through the line over yonder—" He led away from the road, through the trampled wheat to his right, away from the shelling. This was really No Man's Land, for the line curved back from the wood, and thrust out again along the line of another crest, also wooded. Such intervals were watched by day and patrolled by night, and ration parties, carrying details, and other wretches who had

Bringing in German prisoners at St. Mihiel.
Drawn on the field by Captain Thomason.

to traverse them always sweated mightily and anticipated exciting incidents. It was full of smells and mysterious horrors in the starlight, that wheat. Once the platoon came upon a pig, feeding unspeakably. . . . The woods ahead grew plain; the men walked gingerly, straining their eyes at the shadows. . . . "Eighth machine-gun in there—take it easy, you—risky business, this—wish to God I'd—" The platoon stopped, frozen, as they heard the charging handle of a Hotchkiss snick back. A small, sharp voice barked: "Halt—

Ration parties . . . always sweated mightily and anticipated exciting incidents. . . .

who' there?"—"Platoon of the 49th—can we get through here?" "My God, I dam' near gave you a clip! What the hell, comin' up here—don't you know you ain't supposed to come bustin' around a machine-gun position you—" "All right—all right!—shellin' the road down there"—and the platoon scuttled past the Hotchkiss gun, while its crew reviled them. Machine-gunners are a touchy lot, prone to shoot first and inquire afterward; the platoon gave thanks for a man who didn't scare.

They turned left now, and went swiftly through the woods northwest of Lucy. They passed a place where the midnight harassing fire had caught a ration party; a shell had hit a pushcart loaded with loaves of the round French war bread which was the main item of the ration on this front; bread was scattered over an acre or so, and a frenzied sergeant was routing his ration party out of several holes and trying to collect it again. Otherwise, an outfit up in the Bois de Belleau wouldn't eat for another twenty-four hours. The platoon was amused. They took the road to La Voie du Chatelle, stepping out. They'd be well behind the usual shelling, if the Boche was on schedule. Far enough back to talk now, and relax their hunched shoulders.

Down the road they heard a trampling, and the wind brought a smell of unwashed men. "Hi! Relief of Frogs comin' in—!" "Yeh—Frogs. They smell like camels. We smell like goats." "Hope this relief carries a bath wit' it! Me, I've got blue mould all up my back." "Well, next time we come in, we'll put showers in that goddam place. Been there long enough to, already—" "How long we been there?—Le's see—this is the 5th of July, ain't it?—" "Je's, I don't keep count of no days! I can't remember when we was anywhere else—" This was in a tone so mournful that the file's neighbors laughed. "What you doin' in this war, anyway? Dam' replacement, jus' joined up after Hill 142 —" "Man," said the file very earnestly, "I'll tell you. So help me Gawd, I wuz dodgin' the draft!"

The French column came up and passed. Its horizon-blue uniform was invisible in the dark, but the stars glinted a little on its helmets and bayonets. "V'la! Yanquis! B'soir, Americains!" "Dam' right, Frenchie! Bon chance, huh?" They went on without lagging, well closed up. A man's feet dragged going in; there are no such things on a battle-field as fresh troops, for you always approach by forced marches, infinitely weary—"but comin' out —boy, we make knots!—" They reached La Voie du Chatelle, where Regimental was, and there the old Boche always shelled. It was a little farm, pretty well knocked to pieces now, but Regimental was reported to prefer it to a change; they had the Boche's system down so that they could count on him. His shelling always fell into method when he had long enough, and the superior man could, by watching him a few days, avoid unpleasantness. La Voie du Chatelle, as the world knew, received his attention from 11.45 to 12.10 every night. Then he laid off until 3, when his day-shift came on. You could set your watch by it. The platoon went cheerfully past.

A full kilometre farther they hiked, at a furious pace. Then the lieutenant considered that they might catch a rest; they had come a long way and were in a safe spot. Ten minutes' rest out of every hour was the rule when possible. He passed the word: "Fall out to the right of the road," and sat down himself, a little way off, feeling for his chewing-tobacco. You didn't smoke on the front at night—lights were not safe. And chewin' was next best. Then he observed that the platoon was not falling out. They stood in groups on the road, and an angry mutter reached him. "What th'ell?—Goin' out, an' then he wants to rest!" "Yeh, 'fall out on the right of the road,' he says, the goddam fool—" The lieutenant knew his men, as you know men you live in hell with. He got up, chuckling.—"Well, if that's the way you feel about it—come on, you birds!" and he set them a killing step, at which no man complained.

The dawn was coming when they rendezvoused with the battalion in Bois Gros-Jean—beans for breakfast, and hot coffee, and tins of jam! That afternoon they had off their clothes for the first time in three weeks or so, and swam in the Marne at a place called Croutte. And at formation they heard this order published:

VI Armée
Etat-Major
6930/2   Au QGA le 30 Juin, 1918.

In view of the brilliant conduct of the 4th Brigade of
the 2nd U.S. Division, which in a spirited fight took
Bouresches and the important strong point of Bois de
Belleau, stubbornly defended by a large enemy force, the
General commanding the VIth Army orders that, hence-
forth, in all official papers, the Bois de Belleau shall be
named "Bois de la Brigade de Marine."

> The General of Division Degoutte
> Commanding VIth Army
> (Signed) DEGOUTTE.

"Yeh," said the battalion. "Now, about this liberty in
Paris —" But they didn't go to Paris. They took a road that
led through Soissons, and St. Mihiel, and Blanc Mont, and
the Argonne-Meuse, to Nieuwied, on the far side of the
Rhine.

SONGS

ONE

"BANG AWAY, LULU"

The Marines have a very noble song: the Marine Corps Hymn. It is taught, along with close order drill and things like that, to recruits at Parris Island and on the West Coast. It begins:

"From the Halls of Montezuma
To the shores of Tripoli,
We have fought our country's battles
On the land and on the sea . . ."

and it closes, gloriously:

"If the Army and the Navy
Ever look on heaven's scenes,
They will find the streets are guarded
By United States Marines . . ."

This platoon, however, led by a brazen-throated gunnery sergeant, is roaring out:

"Bang away, Lulu . . ."

In the town of Villers-Nancy, where the battalion billeted, they published this order to the troops:

No. 862'3
Ordre Général No. 318

Xe Armée
Etat-Major
3e Bureau   AuQGA 30 July 18

*Officers, Non-Commissioned Officers and Soldiers
of the Third United States Army Corps:*

Shoulder to shoulder with your French comrades you were thrown into the counter-offensive battle which commenced on the 18th of July. You rushed to the attack as to a festival. Your magnificent courage completely routed a surprised enemy and your indomitable tenacity checked the counter-attacks of his fresh divisions. You have shown yourselves worthy sons of your great country, and you were admired by your comrades-in-arms.

Ninety-one guns, 7,200 prisoners, immense booty, 10 kilomètres of country liberated; this is your portion of the spoil of this victory. Furthermore, you have demonstrated your superiority over the barbarian enemy of all mankind. To attack him is to vanquish him.

American comrades! I am grateful to you for the blood so generously spilled on the soil of my country. I am proud to have commanded you during such days, and to have fought with you for the deliverance of the world.

(Signed)   MANGIN.

THE CHARGE AT SOISSONS

THE 1ST Battalion lay in Croutte-sur-Marne. It drank deep of the golden July weather, and swam noisily in the Marne, which swung a blue and shining loop below the town. The battalion took but little interest in the war, which could be heard growling and muttering intermittently to the north and east. Indeed, the unpleasant Bois-de-Belleau-Bouresches area was only a few hours' march distant, and Château-Thierry was just up the river. The guns were loud and continuous in that direction.

But the 2d American Division — Marines and troops of the Regular Army — had just finished a hitch of some thirty-eight days attacking and holding and attacking again, from Hill 142, on the left, through that ghastly wood which the French now called the "Bois de la Brigade de Marine," to Vaux, on the right; and in this battalion, as in the other units of the division, such men as had survived were quite willing to think about something else.

Division Headquarters were over Montreuil way, and thither certain distinguished individuals were ordered, to return with crosses on their faded blouses. This furnished pleasant food for gossip and speculation. Then, vin rouge and vin blanc were to be had, as well as fresh milk for the less carnally minded, and such supplements to the ration were always matters of interest. Also, there were certain buxom mademoiselles among the few civilian families who lingered here in the teeth of the war, and although every girl was watched by lynx-eyed elders early and late, their very presence was stimulating and they were all inclined to be friendly.

The most delightful diversion of all was discussion of the rumor that rose up and ran through the companies: "Got it hot from a bird that was talkin' to a dog-robber at Brigade H. Q.—the division is gonna be sent back to St. Denis for a month's rest, an' leaves, an' everything!" "Yeh! we gonna parade in Paris, too." It was ascertained that St. Denis was right near Paris. Platoon commanders were respectfully approached: "Beggin' the lootenant's pardon, but does the lootenant think that we—" The lieutenants looked wise and answered vaguely and asked the captains. All ranks hung upon the idea.

July 14 came. "Sort o' Frog Fourth o' July," explained a learned corporal, standing in line for morning chow.

"In Paris, they's parades, an' music, an' fireworks, an' all that kinder thing. Speakin' an' barbecues, like back home. Celebratin' the time the Frogs rose agin 'em an' tore down some noted brig or other they had. Now, if I wuz in Paree now, sittin' in front of the Caffey de Pay——!"

"Don't try to go there, Corp. J'seen the cellar they's got fer a brig here?— If you——"

"Don't see no flag-wavin' or such celebrations here. Seen one little Frog kid with his gas-mask an' a Frog flag down the street—no more. Why back home, even in tank towns like this, on the Fourth——"

As a matter of fact, Croutte took on this day no especial joy in the far-off fall of the Bastille. Croutte was in range of the Boche heavy artillery; one could perceive, at the end of this street where, in effect, the house of M'sieu' le Maire had been! An obus of two hundred and twenty centimètres. And others, regard you, near the bridge. Some descended into the river, the naughty ones, and killed many fish. Also, the avions——

Did it not appear to Messieurs les Officers that the cannon were louder this day, especially toward Rheims? And as the day went on, it did appear so. In the afternoon a Boche came out of a cloud and shot down in flames the fat

observation balloon that lived just up the river from
Croutte. The rumor of St. Denis and fourteen-day leaves
waned somewhat. Certainly there grew to be a feeling in
the air. . . .

About one o'clock in the morning of the 15th the Boche
dropped nine-inch shells into the town. The battalion was
turned out, and stood under arms in the dark while the
battalion gas officer sniffed around busily to see if the shells
were the gas variety. They were not, but the battalion,
after the shelling stopped and the casualties were attended
to, observed that in the east a light not of the dawn was
putting out the stars. The eastern sky was all aflame with
gun-flashes, and a growing thunder shook the still air.

The files remarked that they were glad not to be where
all that stuff was lightin', and after breakfast projected the
usual swimming parties. Aquatic sports were then vetoed
by regretful platoon commanders, since it appeared that
Battalion H. Q. had directed the companies to hold themselves in readiness for instant movement to an unspecified
place. Thereupon the guns eastward took on a more than
professional interest. The civilians looked and listened also.
Their faces were anxious. They had heard that noise before.
The hot July hours passed; the battalion continued to be
held in readiness, and got practically no sleep in consequence. There was further shelling, and the guns were undoubtedly louder—and nearer.

Breakfast on the 16th was scant, and the cooks held out
little encouragement for lunch. Lunch was an hour early,
and consisted of beans. "Boys, we're goin' somewhere. We
always gets beans to make a hike on." "Yeh! an' you always
gets more than two-men rates—standin' in line for fourths,
now!"—"What's that sergeant yellin' about—fill yo' canteens? Gonna get ving blonk in mine!"

At noon, the rolling kitchens packed up and moved off,
nobody knew where. The battalion regarded their depar-
ture soberly. "Wish I hadn't et my reserve rations. . . ." The

shadows were lengthening when the bugles blew "assembly" and the companies fell in, taking the broad white road that led down the river. At the next town—towns were thick along the Marne from Château-Thierry to Meaux—they passed through the other battalions of the 5th Marines, jeeringly at ease beside the road. Greetings were tossed about, and the files gibed at each other. "Where you bums goin'?" "Dunno—don't care—But you see the ole 1st Battalion is leadin', as usual!" "Aw—... Close up! close up!"

Beyond them was the 6th Regiment of Marines, arms stacked in the fields by the river. Each battalion took the road in turn, and presently the whole Marine Brigade was swinging down the Marne in the slanting sunlight. Very solid and businesslike the brigade was, keen-faced and gaunt and hard from the great fight behind them, and fit and competent for greater battles yet to come. The companies were under strength, but they had the quality of veterans. They had met the Boche and broken him, and they knew they could do it again. The rumble of the guns was behind them, and the rumor of the leave area still ran strong enough to maintain a slow volubility among the squads. They talked and laughed, but they did not sing. Veterans do not sing a great deal.

It was getting dusk when the 1st Battalion of the 5th, leading, rounded a turn in the road and came upon an endless column of camions, drawn up along the river road as far as one could see. The companies became silent.

"Camions! They rode us to Chatto-Terry in them busses —" "Yeh! an' it was a one-way trip for a hell of a lot of us, too!" "Close up! Close up an' keep to the right of the road."

"Camions! That's a sign they want us bad, somewhere on the line," commented the lean first lieutenant who hiked at the head of the 49th Company. "Walter"—to the officer beside him—"I wonder what happened yesterday an' to-day, with all that shooting." "Don't know—but this

Château-Thierry salient is mighty deep an' narrow, unless
the Boche spread himself yesterday. . . . If we were to break
into it, up near one of the corners . . ." "Yes! Well, we're
right on the tip of it here—can jump either way—Lord!
there's a lot of these conveyances."

Later the battalion knew what had happened on July 15,
when the Boche made his final cast across the Champagne
country toward Rheims and Epernay; and his storm divisions surged to the Marne, and stayed, and lapped around
the foot of the gray Mountain of Rheims, and stayed. Just
now the battalion cared for none of these things. It had no
supper; it faced a crowded trip of uncertain duration, and
was assured of various discomforts after that.

Well accustomed to the ways of war, the men growled
horribly as they crammed into their appointed chariots,
while the officers inexorably loaded the best part of a platoon into each camion, the dusk hiding their grins of sympathy. "Get aboard! get aboard! Where'll you put yo'
pack? Now what the hell do I know about yo' pack—want
a special stateroom an' a coon vallay, do yuh, yuh—!" The
sergeants didn't grin. They swore, and the men swore, and
they raged altogether. But, in much less time than it took
to tell about it afterward, the men were loaded on. The
officers were skilled and prompt in such matters.

Wizened Annamites from the colonies of France drove
the camions. Presently, with clangor and much dust, they
started their engines, and the camion train jolted off down
the river road. A red moon shone wanly through the haze.
The Marne was a silver thread through the valley of a
dream, infinitely aloof from the gasoline-smelling tumult.
. . . "Valley of the Marne! . . . the Marne . . . some of us will
not see you again. . . ."

A camion, as understood by the French, is a motor-
vehicle with small wheels and no springs to speak of. It finds
every hole in the road, and makes an unholy racket; but
it covers ground, the roadbed being of no consequence, as

The automatic-rifle men.

the suffering files bore witness. To the lieutenant of the
49th, nursing his cane on the driver's seat of a lurching
camion, beside two Annamitish heathen who smelt like
camels and chattered like monkeys, came scraps of conversation from the compressed platoon behind him. "Sardines
is comfortable to what we is! . . ." "Chevawz forty—
hommes eight! Lord forgive me, I uster kick about them
noble box cars. . . ." ". . . They say it wuz taxicabs an'
motortrucks that won the first battle of the Marne—yeh!
If they rushed them Frogs up packed like this, you know
they felt like fightin' when they got out!" . . . "I feel like
fightin' now!—take yo' laigs outer my shortribs, you big
embus-kay."

"Night before last they shelled us, an' we stood by last
night—when do we sleep?—that's what I wanna know—"
But sleeping isn't done in camions. The dust on the road
rose thick and white around the train, and rode with it
through the night. The face of the moon, very old and
wise, peered down through the dust. They left the river,
and by the testimony of the stars it seemed to the lieutenant that they were hurrying north. Always, on the
right, the far horizon glowed with the fires of war—flares,
signal-lights, gun-flashes from hidden batteries; the route
paralleled the line. The lieutenant visualized his map: "Fol-
lowin' the salient around—to the north—the north—Soissons way, or Montdidier. . . . The Boche took Soissons. . . ."

Quiet French villages along the road, stone houses like
gray ghosts under the pale moon, and all lights hooded
against Boche planes. Long, empty stretches of road. Shad-
owy columns of French infantry, overtaken and passed.
Horse-drawn batteries of 75s on the move. Swift staff cars
that dashed by, hooting. Then, long files of horsemen,
cloaked and helmeted, with a ghostly glint of lanceheads
over them—French cavalry. Presently, dawn, with low
clouds piling up in the rosy sky. And along the road, wherever there were groves, more cavalry was seen, at ease under

the trees. Horses were picketed, lances and sabres stuck into the ground, and cooking-fires alight.

The Marines had not met the French horse before. They now looked approvingly upon them. Men and horses were alike big and well-conditioned. All morning the camions passed through a country packed with troops and guns, wherever there was cover from the sky. Something big was in the air.

It was mid-forenoon when the train stopped, and the battalion climbed out on cramped legs. "Fall in on the right of the road. . . . Platoon commanders, report. . . . Keep fifty yards' distance between platoons. . . . Squads right. . . . March!" and the companies moved off stiffly, on empty stomachs. The little dark Annamites watched the files pass with incurious eyes. They had taken many men up to battle.

II

Company by company, the 1st Battalion passed on, and behind them the other battalions of the 5th Marines took the road and, after them, the 6th. "None of the wagons, or the galleys—don't see the machine-gun outfits, either," observed the lieutenant of the 49th Company, looking back from the crest of the first low hill. Here the battalion was halted, having marched for half an hour, to tighten slings and settle equipment for the real business of hiking. "They may get up to-night, chow an' all—wonder how far we came, an' where we're goin'. No, sergeant—can't send for water here—my canteen's empty, too. All I know about it is that we seem to be in a hurry."

The dust of the ride had settled thick, like fine gray masks, on the men's faces, and one knew that it was just as thick in their throats! Of course the canteens, filled at Croutte, were finished. The files swore through cracked lips.

The battalion moved off again, and the major up forward

Prussians from Von Boehn's divisions in and around the Bois de Belleau.
A page from Captain Thomason's sketch-book.

set a pace all disproportionate to his short legs. When the
first halt came, the usual ten-minute rest out of the hour
was cut to five. "Aw hell! forced march!" "An' the
lootenant has forgot everything but 'close up' close up!'
—Listen at him——"

The camions had set them down in a gently rolling
country, unwooded, and fat with ripening wheat. Far
across it, to the north, blue with distance, stood a great
forest, and toward this forest the battalion marched, talk-
ative, as men are in the first hour of the hike, before the
slings of the pack begin to cut into your shoulders. . . .
"Look at them poppies in the wheat."—"They ain't as red
as the poppies were the mornin' of the 6th of June, when
we went up Hill 142—" "Yep! Beginnin' to fade some. It's
gettin' late in the season." "Hi—I'm beginnin' to fade some
myself—this guerre is wearin' on a man . . . remember how
they looked in the wheat that mornin', just before we hit
the Maxim guns?—red as blood—" "Pore old Jerry Finnegan picked one and stuck it in the buckle of his helmet—
I seen it in his tin hat after he was killed, there behin' the
Hill. . . . I'll always think about poppies an' blood together,
as long as I live—" This last from little Tritt, the lieutenant's orderly.

"Long as you live—that's good!" gibed Corporal Snair,
of the Company Headquarters group. "Don't you know by
now how expendable you bucks are?"—The lieutenant
heard, and remembered it, oddly enough, in a crowded
moment the next day, when he lost the two of them to a
hard-fought Maxim gun.

No wind moved across the lonely wheatland; the bearded
stalks waved not at all, and the sun-drenched air was hot
and dead. Sweat made muddy runnels through the thick
white dust that masked the faces of the men. Conversation
languished; what was said was in profane monosyllables.
Clouds came up, and there were showers of rain, with hot
sunshine between. Uniforms steamed after each shower,

and thirst became a torture. The man who had the vin
blanc in his canteen fell out and was quite ill. "Hikin'—
in—a dam'—Turkish bath—"

After interminable hours, the column came to the forest and passed from streaming sunshine into sultry shades.
It was a noble wood of great high-branching trees, clean of
underbrush as a park. Something was doing in the forest.
Small-arms ammunition was stacked beside the road, and
there were dumps of shells and bombs under the trees. And
French soldiers everywhere. This road presently led into a
great paved highway, and along it were more of the prop-
erties of war—row upon row of every caliber of shell,
orderly stacks of winged aerial bombs, pile after pile of
rifle and machine-gun ammunition, and cases of handgrenades and pyrotechnics. There were picket-lines of cavalry,
and park after park of artillery, light and heavy. There
were infantrymen with stacked rifles.

Gunner and horseman and poilu, they looked amicably
upon the sweating Marines, and waved their hands with
naïve Gallic friendliness. The battalion came out of its
weariness and responded in kind. "Say, where do they get
that stuff about little Frenchmen? Look at that long-
sparred soldier yonder—seven feet if he's an inch!"—
"Them gunners is fine men, too. All the runts in the Frog
army is in the infantry!"—"Well, if these Frawgs fights
accordin' to their size, Gawd pity the old Boche when that
cavalry gets after him—lances an' all!" "You said it! Them
little five-foot-nothin' infantry, with enough on their
backs, in the way o' tents an' pots an' pans, to set up light
housekeepin' wit, and that long squirrel gun they carry,
an' that knittin-needle bayonet—! Remember how they
charged at Torcy, there on the left——?"

The French were cooking dinner beside the road. For
your Frenchman never fights without his kitchens and a
full meal under his cartridge-pouches. They go into the
front line with him, the kitchens and the chow, and there

is always the coffee avec rhum, and the good hot soup that smells so divinely to the hungry Americans, passing empty. "When we goes up to hit the old Boche, we always says adoo to the galleys till we comes out again—guess the idea is to starve us so we'll be mad, like the lions in them glad-i-a-tor-ial mills the corp'ril was tellin' about."—"Hell! we don't eat, it seems—them Frawgs might at least have the decency to keep their home cookin' where we can't smell it!"

The highway led straight through the forest. Many roads emptied into it, and from every road debouched a stream of horses, men, and guns. The battalion went into column of twos, then into column of files, to make room. On the left of the road, abreast of the Marines, plodded another column of foot—strange black men, in the blue greatcoats of the French infantry and mustard-yellow uniforms under them. Their helmets were khaki-colored, and bore a crescent instead of the bursting bomb of the French line. But they marched like veterans, and the Marines eyed them approvingly. Between the foot, the road was level-full of guns and transport, moving axle to axle, and all moving in the same direction. In this column were tanks, large and small, all ring-streaked and striped with camouflage, mounting one-pounders and machine-guns; and the big ones, short-barrelled 75s.

The tanks were new to the Marines. They moved with a horrific clanging and jangling, and stunk of petrol. "Boy, what would you do if you seen one of them little things comin' at you? The big ones is males, and the little ones is females, the lootenant says. . . ." "Chillun, we're goin' into somethin' big—Dunno what, but it's big!"

The sultry afternoon passed wearily, and at six o'clock the battalion turned off the road, shambling and footsore, and rested for two hours. They found water and filled canteens. A few of the hardier made shift to wash. "Gonna smear soapsuds an' lather all over me—the Hospital Corps men say it keeps off mustard-gas!" But most of the men dropped where the platoon broke ranks and slept. Battalion H. Q. sent for all company commanders.

Presently the lieutenant of the 49th returned, with papers and a map. He called the company officers around him, and spread the map on the ground. He spoke briefly.

"We're in the Villers-Cotterets woods—the Forêt de Retz. At H hour on D day, which I think is to-morrow morning, although the major didn't say, we attack the Boche here"—pointing—"and go on to here—past the town of Vierzy. Eight or nine kilomètres. Three objectives —marked—so—and so. The 2nd Division with one of the infantry regiments leading, and the 5th Marines, attacks with the 1st Moroccan Division on our left. The Frog Foreign Legion is somewhere around too, and the 1st American Division. It's Mangin's Colonial Army—the bird they call the butcher.

"The 49th Company has the division's left, and we're to keep in touch with the French over there. They're Senegalese—the niggers you saw on the road, and said to be bon fighters. The tanks will come behind us through the woods, and take the lead as soon as we hit the open.

"No special instructions, except, if we are held up any place, signal a tank by wavin' a rag or something on a bayonet, in the direction of the obstacle, and the tank will do the rest.

"No rations, an' we move soon. See that canteens are filled. Now go and explain it all to your platoons, and— better take a sketch from this map—it's the only one I have. Impress it on everybody that the job is to maintain connection between the Senegalese on the left and our people. Tritt, I'm goin' to catch a nap—wake me when we move——"

It was dark when the battalion fell in and took the road again. They went into single file on the right, at the very

"Keep on to the left until you meet the Moroccans, and go forward. . . ." 4.30 A. M., July 18, 1918.

edge of it, for the highway was jammed with three columns of traffic, moving forward. It began to rain, and the
night, there under the thick branches, was inconceivably
black. The files couldn't see the man ahead, and each man
caught hold of the pack in front and went feeling for the
road with his feet, clawing along with the wheels and the
artillery horses and machine-gun mules. On the right was
a six-foot ditch, too deep in mud to march in. The rain
increased to a sheeted downpour and continued all night,
with long rolls of thunder, and white stabs of lightning
that intensified the dark. The picked might of France and
America toiled on that road through the Villers-Cotterets
forest that night, like a great flowing river of martial force.

And after the 5th Marines have forgotten the machine-
guns that sowed death in the wheat behind Hill 142, and
the shrapnel that showered down at Blanc Mont, before St.
Etienne, they will remember the march to the Soissons battle, through the dark and the rain. . . .

As guns and caissons slewed sideways across the files, or
irate machine-gun mules plunged across the tangle, the
column slowed and jammed and halted on heavy feet; then
went on again to plunge blindly against the next obstacle.
Men fell into the deep ditch and broke arms and legs. Just
to keep moving was a harder test than battle ever imposed.
The battalion was too tired to swear. I'm to where—I have
to think about movin' my feet—! Plant—the left foot—an'
—advance the right—an'—bring up the—left foot—
an'——"

No battle ever tried them half as hard as the night road
to Soissons. . . .

The rain ceased, and the sky grew gray with dawn. The
traffic thinned, and the battalion turned off on a smaller
road, closed up, and hurried on. Five minutes by the side
of the road to form combat packs and strip to rifle and
bayonet. "Fall in quickly! Forward!"

Overhead the clouds were gone; a handful of stars paled

and went out; day was coming. The battalion, lightened, hastened. They perceived, dimly, through a mist of fatigue, that a cloudless day was promised and that the world was wonderfully new washed and clean—and quiet! Not a gun anywhere, and the mud on the road muffled the sound of hobnailed boots. "Double time! Close up! Close up, there!"

There had been fighting here; there were shell-holes, scarred and splintered trees. The battalion panted to a crossroads, where stone buildings lay all blasted by some gale of shell-fire. And by the road what looked like a well! The files swayed toward it, clutching at dry canteens— "Back in ranks! Back in ranks, you——!"

Then, barbed wire across the roadway, and battered shallow trenches to right and left, and a little knot of French and American officers, Major Turrill standing forward. The leading company turned off to the left, along the trenches. The 49th followed in column. "Turn here," ordered the major. "Keep on to the left until you meet the Moroccans, and go forward. . . ." The 49th went beyond the trench, still in column of route, picking its way through the woods. The lieutenant looked back at his men as he went; their faces were gray and drawn and old; they were staggering with weariness—"Fix bayonets—" and the dry click of the steel on the locking-ring ran along the ragged column, loud in the hush of dawn.

III

It was 4:35, the morning of July 18.

Miles of close-laid batteries opened with one stupendous thunder. The air above the tree-tops spoke with unearthly noises, the shriek and rumble of light and heavy shells. Forward through the woods, very near, rose up a continued crashing roar of explosions, and a murk of smoke, and a hell of bright fires continually renewed. It lasted only five minutes, that barrage, with every French and American gun that could be brought to bear firing to top speed. But

Listening-post rushed by Senegalese.

they were terrible minutes for the unsuspecting Boche. Dazed, beaten down, and swept away, he tumbled out of his holes when it lifted, only to find the long bayonets of the Americans licking like flame across his forward positions, and those black devils, the Senegalese, raging with knives in his rifle-pits. His counter-barrage was slow and weak, and when it came the shells burst well behind the assaulting waves which were already deep in his defenses.

The 49th Company, running heavily, sodden with weariness, was plunging through a line of wire entanglements when the guns opened. A French rifleman squatted in a hole under the wire, and a sergeant bent over him and shouted: "Combien—how far—damn it, how you say?—combien—kilomètre—à la Boche?" The Frenchman's eyes bulged. He did violent things with his arms. "Kilomèt'? *kilomètres?* Mon Dieu, cent mètres! Cent mètres!" Half the company, still in column, was struggling in the wire when, from the tangle right in front, a machine-gun dinned fiercely and rifle-fire ran to left and right through the woods.

It was well that the woods were a little open in that spot, so that the lieutenant's frantic signals could be seen, for no voice could have been heard. And it was more than well that every man there had been shot over enough not to be gun-shy. They divined his order, they deployed to the left, and they went forward yelling. That always remained, to the lieutenant, the marvel of the Soissons fight—how those men, two days without food, three nights without sleep, after a day and a night of forced marching, flung off their weariness like a discarded piece of equipment, and at the shouting of the shells sprang fresh and eager against the German line.

Liaison—to keep the touch—was his company's mission —the major's last order. To the left were only the smoky woods—no Senegalese in sight—and to the left the lieutenant anxiously extended his line, throwing out the last two platoons, while the leading one shot and stabbed among

the first Boche machine-guns. He himself ran in that direction, cursing and stumbling in wire and fallen branches,
having no time for certain Boches who fired at him over a
bush. . . . Finally, Corbett, the platoon commander, leading
to the left, turned and waved his arms. And through the
trees he saw the Senegalese—lean, rangy men in mustard-
colored uniforms, running with their bayonets all aslant.
He turned back toward his company with the sweetest feeling of relief that he had ever known; he had his contact
established; his clever and war-wise company would attend
to keeping it, no matter what happened to him.

The battle roared into the wood. Three lines of machine-
guns, echeloned, held it. Here the Forêt de Retz was like
Dante's wood, so shattered and tortured and horrible it was,
and the very trees seemed to writhe in agony. Here the fury
of the barrage was spent, and the great trunks, thick as a
man's body, were sheared off like weed-stalks; others were
uprooted and lay gigantic along the torn earth; big limbs
still crashed down or swayed half-severed; splinters and
débris choked the ways beneath. A few German shells fell
among the men—mustard-gas; and there in the wet woods
one could see the devilish stuff spreading slowly, like a
snaky mist, around the shell-hole after the smoke had
lifted.

Machine-guns raved everywhere; there was a crackling
din of rifles, and the coughing roar of hand-grenades. Company and platoon commanders lost control—their men
were committed to the fight—and so thick was the going
that anything like formation was impossible. It was every
man for himself, an irregular, unbroken line, clawing
through the tangles, climbing over fallen trees, plunging
heavily into Boche rifle-pits. Here and there a well-fought
Maxim gun held its front until somebody—officer, non-
com, or private—got a few men together and, crawling to
left or right, gained a flank and silenced it. And some guns
were silenced by blind, furious rushes that left a trail of

A fighting swirl of Senegalese.

writhing khaki figures, but always carried two or three frenzied Marines with bayonets into the emplacement; from whence would come shooting and screaming and other clotted unpleasant sounds, and then silence.

From such a place, with four men, the lieutenant climbed, and stood leaning on his rifle, while he wiped the sweat from his eyes with a shaking hand. Panting, white or red after their nature—for fighting takes men differently, as whiskey does—the four grouped around him. One of them squatted and was very sick. And one of them, quite young and freckled, explored a near-by hole and prodded half a dozen Boches out of it, who were most anxious to make friends. The other three took interest in this, and the Boches saw death in their eyes. They howled like animals, these big hairy men of Saxony, and capered in a very ecstasy of terror. The freckled Marine set his feet deliberately, judging his distance, and poised his bayonet. The lieutenant grasped his arm—"No! No! take 'em back—they've quit. Take 'em to the rear, I tell you!" The freckled one obeyed, very surly, and went off through the tangle to the rear. The lieutenant turned and went on.

To left and right he caught glimpses of his men, running, crawling, firing as they went. In a clearing, Lieutenant Appelgate, of the 17th Company, on the right, came into view. He waved his pistol and shouted something. He was grinning. . . . All the men were grinning . . . it was a bon fight, after all. . . .

Then little Tritt, his orderly, running at his side, went down, clawing at a bright jet of scarlet over his collar. The war became personal again—a keening sibilance of flesh-hunting bullets, ringing under his helmet. He found himself prone behind a great fallen tree, with a handful of his men; bark and splinters were leaping from the round trunk that sheltered them.

"You"—to a panting half-dozen down the log—"crawl

back to the stump and shoot into that clump of green
bushes over there, where you see the new dirt—it's in there!
Everything you've got, and watch for me up ahead.
Slover"—to Sergeant Robert Slover, a small, fiery man
from Tennessee—"come on."

They crawled along the tree. Back toward the stump the
Springfields crackled furiously. Somewhere beyond the
machine-gun raved like a mad thing, and the Boches around
it threw handgrenades that made much smoke and noise.
The two of them left the protection of the trunk, and felt
remarkably naked behind a screen of leaves. They crawled
slowly, stopping to peer across at the bushes. The lieutenant
caught the dull gleam of a round gray helmet, moved a
little, and saw the head and the hands of the Boche who
worked the gun. He pushed the sergeant with his foot and,
moving very carefully, got his rifle up and laid his cheek
against the stock. Over his sights, the German's face,
twenty metres away, was intent and serious. The lieutenant
fired, and saw his man half-rise and topple forward on
the gun.

Then things happened fast. Another German came into
view straining to tear the fallen gunner off the firing mech-
anism. Slover shot him. There was another, and another.
Then the bush boiled like an ant-heap, and a feldwebel
sprang out with a grenade, which he did not get to throw.
It went off, just the same, and the Marines from the other
end of the tree came with bayonets. . . . Presently they went
on. . . . "There's a squad of them bastards to do orderly
duty for the corp'ral an' little Tritt," said the sergeant.
"Spread out more, you birds."

Afterward, sweating and panting, the freckled one who
had started back with prisoners caught up with the lieutenant. "Lootenant, sir!" he gasped, wiping certain stains
from his bayonet with his sleeve. "Them damn Heinies
tried to run on me, an' I jest natcherly had to shoot 'em up

Fighting from tree to tree in the woods south of Soissons.
A chaut-chaut automatic rifle in action.

a few—" and he looked guilelessly into the officer's eyes. "Why you—Hell! . . . fall in behind me, then, an' come along. Need another orderly."

He pondered absently on the matter of frightfulness as he picked his way along. There were, in effect, very few prisoners taken in the woods that morning. It was close-up, savage work. "But speakin' of frightfulness, one of these nineteen-year-olds, with never a hair to his face—" A spitting gust of machine-gun bullets put an end to extraneous musings.

Later, working to the left of his company, he was caught up in a fighting swirl of Senegalese and went with them into an evil place of barbed wire and machine-guns. These wild black Mohammedans from West Africa were enjoying themselves. Killing, which is at best an acquired taste with the civilized races, was only too palpably their mission in life. Their eyes rolled, and their splendid white teeth flashed in their heads, but here all resemblance to a happy Southern darky stopped. They were deadly. Each platoon swept its front like a hunting-pack, moving swiftly and surely together. The lieutenant felt a thrill of professional admiration as he went with them.

The hidden guns that fired on them were located with uncanny skill; they worked their automatic rifles forward on each flank until the doomed emplacement was under a scissors fire; then they took up the matter with the bayonet, and slew with lion-like leaps and lunges and a shrill barbaric yapping. They took no prisoners. It was plain that they did not rely on rifle-fire or understand the powers of that arm—to them a rifle was merely something to stick a bayonet on—but with the bayonet they were terrible, and the skill of their rifle grenadiers and automatic-rifle men always carried them to close quarters without too great loss.

They carried also a broad-bladed knife, razor-sharp, which disembowelled a man at a stroke. The slim bayonet of the French breaks off short when the weight of a body pulls down and sidewise on it; and then the knives come out. With reason the Boche feared them worse than anything living, and the lieutenant saw in those woods unwounded fighting Germans who flung down their rifles when the Senegalese rushed, and covered their faces, and stood screaming against the death they could not look upon. And—in a lull, a long, grinning sergeant, with a cruel aquiline face, approached him and offered a brace of human ears, nicely fresh, strung upon a thong. "B'jour, Americain! Voilà! Beaucoup souvenir ici—bon! Désirez-vous? Bon——!"

Later, on the last objective, there was a dignified Boche major of infantry, who came at discretion out of a deep dugout, and spoke in careful English: "Und I peg of you, Herr leutnant, to put me under trusty guard of your Americans true-and-tried! Ja! These black savages, of the art of war most ignorant, they would kill us prave Germans in cold plood! . . . The Herr General Mangin, that"—here a poignant string of gutturals—"I tell you, Herr leutnant, der very name of Mangin, it is equal to fünf divisions on unser front!"

Back with his own men again, the company whittled thin! Was there no limit to the gloomy woods? . . . Light through the trees yonder!——

The wood ended, and the attack burst out into the rolling wheat-land, where the sun shone in a cloudless sky and poppies grew in the wheat. To the right, a great paved road marched, between tall poplars, much battered. On the road two motor-trucks burned fiercely, and dead men lay around them. Across the road a group of stone farm-buildings had been shelled into a smoking dust-heap, but from the ruins a nest of never-die machine-guns opened flanking fire. The khaki lines checked and swirled around them, and there was a mounting crackle of rifle-fire . . . and the bayonets got in. The lines went forward to the low crest beyond, where, astride the road, was the first objective; and

With reason the Boche feared them worse than anything living.

the assault companies halted here to reform. A few Boche shells howled over them, but the Boche was still pounding the wood, where the support battalions followed. The tanks debouched from the forest and went forward through the infantry.

In a hollow just ahead of the reformed line something was being dealt with by artillery, directed by the planes that dipped and swerved above the fight. The shells crashed down and made a great roaring murk of smoke and dust and flickering flames of red and green. The lieutenant, his report to the major despatched, and his company straightened out, along with men from other units and a handful of Senegalese who had attached themselves to him, ran an expert eye along his waiting squads, and allowed his mind to settle profoundly on breakfast. "Let's see—it's July, an' in Texas they'll be having cantaloupes, and coffee, an' eggs, an' bacon an'—" Second Lieutenant Corbett, beside him, groaned like a man shot through the body, and he realized that he had been thinking aloud. Then Corbett seized his arm, and gasped: "Lordy! Look at——"

The shelling forward had abated, but the smoke and murk of it still hung low. Into this murk every man in the line was now peering eagerly. Advancing toward them, dimly seen, was a great body of Germans, hundreds upon hundreds, in mass formation——

Pure joy ran among the men. They took out cartridges, and arranged them in convenient piles. They tested the wind with wetted fingers, and set their sights, and licked their lips. "Range three-fifty—Oh, boy, ain't war wonderful! We been hearin' about this mass-formation stuff, an' now we gets a chance at it——!"

Then: "Aw, hell! Prisoners!" "The low-life bums, they all got their hands up!" "Lookit! One o' them tanks is ridin' herd over them——" It was the garrison of a strong point.

The artillery had battered them, and when it lifted, and they had come out of their holes, they found a brace of agile tanks squatting over their defenses with one-pounders and machine-guns. They had very sensibly surrendered, en masse, and were now ambling through the attacking lines to the rear.

The officers' whistles shrilled, and the attack went on. The woods fell away behind, and for miles to left and right across the rolling country the waves of assault could be seen. It was a great stirring pageant wherein moved all the forces of modern war. The tanks, large and small, lumbered in advance. Over them the battle-planes flew low, searching the ground, rowelling the Boche with bursts of machine-gun fire. The infantry followed close, assault waves deployed, support platoons in column, American Marines and Regulars, Senegalese and the Foreign Legion of France, their rifles slanting forward, and the sun on all their bayonets. And behind the infantry, straining horses galloped with lean-muzzled 75s, battery on battery—artillery, over the top at last with the rifles. On the skirts of the attack hovered squadrons of cavalry the Marines had seen the day before, dragoons and lancers, marked from afar by the sparkle and glitter of lance-heads and sabres.

And forward through the wheat, the Boche lines broke and his strong points crumbled; standing stubbornly in one place; running in panic at another; and here and there attempting sharp counter-attacks; but everywhere engulfed; and the battle roared over him. The Boche was in mixed quality that day. Some of his people fought and died fighting; a great many others threw down their arms and bleated "Kamaraden" at the distant approach of the attackers.

The rest was no connected story. Only the hot exaltation of the fight kept the men on their feet. Wheat waist-high is almost as hard to get through as running water, and the sun was pitiless. To the left of the battalion, and forward, machine-guns fired from the Chaudun farm; the 17th Company went in and stamped the Maxims flat. In a little

The fighting in the woods at Soissons was close and savage.

hollow there was a battery of 105s that fired pointblank upon the Marines, the gunners working desperately behind their gun-shields. The Marines worked to right and left and beat them down with rifle-fire, and later a gunnery sergeant and a wandering detachment of Senegalese turned one of these guns around and shelled the Vierzy ravine with it—range 900 yards—to the great annoyance of the Boche in that place.

Further, a hidden strong point in the wheat held them, and a tank came and sat upon that strong point and shot it into nothing with a one-pounder gun. Another place, hidden Saxons, laired behind low trip-wires in high wheat, raked the line savagely. There was crawling and shooting low among the poppies, and presently hand-to-hand fighting, in which the freckled boy saw his brother killed and went himself quite mad among the wounded and the corpses with his bayonet. . . .

Then, without being very clear as to how they got there, the lieutenant and his company and a great many others were at the Vierzy ravine, in the cross-fire of the machine-guns that held it.

The ravine was very deep and very precipitous and wooded. A sunken road led into it and, while the riflemen stalked the place cannily, a tank came up and disappeared down the sunken road. A terrific row of rifles and grenades arose, and a wild yelling. Running forward, the Marines observed that the tank was stalled, its guns not working; and a gray, frantic mass of German infantry was swarming over it, prying at its plates with bayonets and firing into such openings as could be found. One beauty of the tank is that, when it is in such a difficulty, you can fire without fearing for your friends inside. The automatic-rifle men especially enjoyed the brief crowded seconds that followed. Then all at once the farther slope of the ravine swarmed with running Boches, and the Americans knelt or lay down at ease, and fired steadily and without haste. As they passed the tank a greasy, smiling Frenchman emerged head and shoulders and inquired after a cigarette. There were very many dead Germans in the ravine and on its slope when they went forward.

Wearily now, the exaltation dying down, they left the stone towers of Vierzy to the right, in the path of the Regulars of the 9th and 23d. On line northeast of it they halted and prepared to hold. It was a lonesome place. Very thin indeed were the assault companies; very far away the support columns. . . . "Accordin' to the map, we're here. Turn those Boche machine-guns around—guess we'll stay. Thank God, we must have grabbed off all their artillery, 'cept the heavies. . . ."

"Lootenant, come up here, for God's sake! Lord, what a slew o' Boches!" Beyond rifle-shot a strong gray column was advancing. There were machine-guns with it. It was not deployed, but its intention was very evident. . . . Here were thirty-odd Marines and a few strays from one of the infantry regiments—nobody in sight, flanks or rear——

But to the rear a clanging and a clattering, and the thudding of horse-hoofs!—"Graves, beat it back an' flag those guns." Graves run frantically, waving his helmet. The guns halted in a cloud of dust, and a gunner lieutenant trotted up, jaunty, immaculate. He dismounted, in his beautiful pale-blue uniform and his gleaming boots and tiny jingling spurs, and saluted the sweating, unshaven Marine officer. He looked with his glasses, and he consulted his map, and then he smiled like a man who has gained his heart's desire. He dashed back toward his guns, waving a signal.

The guns wheeled around; the horses galloped back; there was a whirl and bustle behind each caisson, and two gunners with a field-telephone came running. It all happened in seconds.

The first 75 barked, clear and incisive, and the shell whined away . . . the next gun, and the next. . . . The little

A Lieutenant of Marines and a German major, hand to hand.

puff-balls, ranging shots, burst very near the Boche column. Then the battery fired as one gun—a long rafale of fire, wherein no single gun could be heard but a drumming thunder.

Smoke and fire flowered hideously over the Boche column. A cloud hit it for a space. When the cloud lifted the column had disintegrated; there was only a far-off swarm of fleeing figures, flailed by shrapnel as they ran. And the glass showed squirming heaps of gray flattened on the ground. . . .

The gunner officer looked and saw that his work was good. "Bon, eh? Soixante-quinze—!" With an all-embracing gesture and a white-toothed smile, he went. Already his battery was limbered up and galloping, and when the first retaliatory shell came from an indignant Boche 155, the 75s were a quarter of a mile away. The Boche shelled the locality with earnestness and method for the next hour, but he did not try to throw forward another column. . . . "Man, I jest love them little 75s! Swa-sont-cans bon? Say, that Frog said a mouthful!"

The lieutenant wrote and sent back his final report: ". . . and final objective reached, position organized at . . ." and stopped and swore in amazement when he looked at his watch—barely noon! Sergeant Cannon's watch corroborated the time— "But, by God! The way my laigs feel, it's day after to-morrow, anyway!—" "Wake those fellows up—got to finish diggin' in—No tellin' what we'll get here—" Some of his people were asleep on their rifles. Some were searching for iron crosses among the dead. A sergeant came with hands and mouth full. "Sir, they's a bunch of this here black German bread and some stuff that looks like coffee, only ain't—in that dugout—" And the company found the Kriegsbrot and Kaffee Ersatz will sustain life, and even taste good if you've been long enough without food. . . .

The shadows turned eastward; in the rear bloated observation balloons appeared on the sky-line. "Them fellers gets a good view from there. Lonesome, though . . ." "Wonder where all our planes went—don't see none—" "Hell! Went home to lunch! Them birds, they don't allow no guerre to interfere with their meals. Now, that's what I got against this fighting stuff—it breaks into your three hots a day." "Boy, I'm so empty I could button my blouse on the knobs of my spine! Hey—yonder's a covey o' them a-vions now— low—strung out—Boche! Hit the deck!"

They were Boche—sinister red-nosed machines that came out of the eye of the sun and harrowed the flattened infantry, swooping one after another with bursts of machine-gun fire. Also they dropped bombs. Some of them went after the observation balloons, and shot more than one down, flaming, before they could be grounded. And not an Ally plane in sight, anywhere! To be just, there was one, in the course of the afternoon; he came from somewhere, and went away very swiftly, with five Germans on his tail. The lieutenant gathered from the conversation of his men that they thought the Frenchman used good judgment.

That afternoon the Boche had the air. He dropped bombs and otherwise did the best he could to make up, with planes, for the artillery that he had lost that morning. On the whole, he was infinitely annoying. There's something about being machine-gunned from the air that gets a man's goat, as the files remarked with profane emphasis. Much futile rifle-fire greeted his machines as they came and went, and away over on the right toward Vierzy the lieutenant saw one low-flying fellow crumple and come down like a stricken duck. This plane, alleged to have been brought down by a chaut-chaut automatic rifle, was afterward officially claimed by four infantry regiments and a machine-gun battalion. Late in the afternoon the French brought up anti-aircraft guns on motor-trucks and the terror of the air abated somewhat; but, while it lasted, the lieutenant heard——

Sketches made by Captain Thomason at Soissons on scraps of paper
taken from a feldwebel's note-book.

"There comes—" (great rending explosion nearby) "Goddamighty! 'nother air-bomb?"

"Naw, thank God! That was only a shell!"

As dusk fell, the French cavalry rode forward through the lines. The lieutenant thoughtfully watched a blue squadron pass— "If spirits walk, Murat and Marshal Ney an' all the Emperor's cavalry are ridin' with those fellows. . . ."

In the early dawn of the next day the cavalry rode back. One squadron went through the company's position. It was a very small squadron, indeed, this morning. Half the troopers led horses with empty saddles. A tall young captain was in command. They were drawn and haggard from the night's work, but the men carried their heads high, and even the horses looked triumphant. They had, it developed, been having a perfectly wonderful time, riding around behind the German lines. They had shot up transport, and set fire to ammunition-dumps, and added greatly to the discomfort of the Boche. They thought they might go back again to-night. . . . They did.

The night of the 19th the galleys got up, and the men had hot food. Early the morning of the 20th the division was relieved and began to withdraw to reserve position, while fresh troops carried the battle on. The 1st Battalion of the 5th Marines marched back, in a misty dawn, across the ground they had fought over two days before. In the trampled fields, where the dead lay unburied, old French territorials were mowing the ripe wheat and shocking it up. The battle was far away. . . .

The battalion entered the woods and turned off the road toward the blue smoke of the galleys, from which came an altogether glorious smell of food. One of the company officers ran ahead of the 49th to find a place to stack arms and pile equipment. Presently he beckoned, and the lieutenant led his people to the place—a sort of clearing, along one side of which lay a great fallen tree. Under an outthrust leafy branch something long and stiff lay covered with a blanket.

"Stack arms . . . fall out!"

Graves, the officer who had gone ahead, was standing by the blanket. "Do you know who's under this?" he said. The lieutenant stooped and looked. It was little Tritt. . . .

Fighting north of Blanc Mont, Champagne

After breakfast, some of the men enlarged the pit where the machine-gun had been and tidied it up. . . . They wrapped the body in a blanket and two German waterproof sheets that were handy, and buried the boy there.

". . . But before he got it, he knew that we were winning." The men put on their helmets and went away, to look for others who had stopped in the woods . . . to gather souvenirs.

"Well, he's where he ain't hungry, an' his feet don't hurt from hikin', an' his heavy marchin' order won't never cut into his shoulders any more. . . ." "No, nor no damn Boche buzzards drop air-bombs on him——"

"Wonder where we'll hit the old Boche next——"

SONGS

TWO

"CARRY ME BACK
TO
OLE VIRGINNY"

The old Boche helmet made an excellent thing to cook with. You jabbed a few holes in it with a bayonet, so's to have a draft, and a mess-kit fitted over it beautifully. When you could get it, strips of high explosive, picked up around a 155-mm. gun position, made the best fuel, giving you a fine, hot, smokeless fire. Smoke was not desirable on the front.

The chap on the opposite page is frying hard bread in bacon grease; he will sprinkle a little beet-sugar on it and have a real delicacy. Filling, too. As he goes about this domestic labor, he is humming "Carry me back to Ole Virginny." But the files in the background are attracted by the smell—not the song.

MARINES AT BLANC MONT

> The taking of Blanc Mont is the greatest single achievement
> of the 1918 campaign—the Battle of Liberation.
>   —MARSHAL PETAIN.

THE BATTALION groped its way through the wet darkness to a wood of scrubby pines, and lay down in the slow autumn rain. North and east the guns made a wall of sound; flashes from hidden batteries and flares sent up from nervous front-line trenches lighted the low clouds; occasional shells from the Boche heavies whined overhead, searching the transport lines to the rear. It lacked an hour yet until dawn, and the companies disposed themselves in the mud and slept. They had learned to get all the sleep they could before battle.

A few days before, this battalion, the first of the 5th Regiment of Marines, a unit of the 2nd Division, had pulled out of a pleasant town below Toul, in the area where the division rested after the Saint-Mihiel drive, and had come north a day and a night by train, to Chalons-sur-Marne. Thence, by night marches, the division had gathered in certain bleak and war-worn areas behind the Champagne front, and here general orders announced that the 2nd was detached from the American forces and lent by the Generalissimo as a special reserve to Gouraud's 4th French Army.

Forthwith arose gossip about General Gouraud, the one-armed and able defender of Rheims, who had broken the German offensive in July. "A big bird with a beak of a nose and one of these here square beards on 'im—holds hisself straighter than the run of Frog generals," confided a motorcycle driver from division headquarters. "Seen him in Challawns. They say he fights."

"Yeh, ole Foch has picked the right babies this time," observed the files complacently. "Special reserve—that's us all over, Mable! Hope they keep us in reserve—but we know they won't! The Frogs have got something nasty they want us to get outa the way for them. An' we see Chasser d'Alpinos and Colonials around here. Somethin' distressin' is just bound to happen."

"Roll your packs, you birds! The lootenant passed the word we're goin' up in camions to-night!"

The battalion got aboard in its turn, just as dusk deepened into dark, rode until the camion train stopped, and marched through the rain to its appointed place.

I

The dawn came very reluctantly through the clouds, bringing no sun with it, although the drizzle stopped. The battalion rose from its soggy blankets, kneading stiffened muscles to restore circulation, and gathered in disconsolate shivering groups around the galleys. These had come up in the night, and from them, standing under the dripping pines, came a promising smell of hot coffee. Something hot was the main consideration in life just now. But the fires were feeble, and something hot was long in coming. The cooks swore because dry wood couldn't be found, and wet wood couldn't be risked, because it would draw shell-fire. The men swore at the weather and the slowness of the kitchen force, and the war in general, and they all growled together.

"Quite right—entirely fitting and proper!" said the second-in-command of the 49th Company, coming up to where his captain gloomed beside the galley. "We wouldn't know what to do with Marines who didn't growl. But, El Capitan, if you'll go over to that ditch yonder, you'll find some Frog artillerymen with a lovely cooking-fire. They gave me hot coffee with much rum in it. A great people, the Frogs—" But the captain was already gone, and the second-in-command, who was a lean first lieutenant in a mouse-colored raincoat, had to run to catch up with him.

They returned in time to see their company and the other companies of the battalion lining up for chow. This matter being disposed of, the men cast incurious eyes about them.

The French artillerymen called the place "the Wood of the Seven Pigeons." There were no pigeons here now. Only hidden batteries of 105s, with their blue-clad attendants huddled in shelters around them. The wood was a sparse growth of scrubby pines that persisted somehow on the long slope of one of the low hills of Suippes, in the sinister Champagne country. Many of the pines were blackened and torn by shell-fire, and the chalky soil was pockmarked with shell craters from Boche counter-battery work, searching for the French guns camouflaged there. Trenches zigzagged through the pines, old and new, with belts of rusty wire. There were graves.

North from the edge of the pines the battalion looked out on desolation where the once grassy, rolling slopes of the Champagne stretched away like a great white sea that had been dead and accursed through all time. Near at hand was Souain, a town of the dead, a shattered skeleton of a place, with shells breaking over it. Beyond and northward was Somme-Py, nearly blotted out by four years of war. From there to the horizon, east and west and north and south, was all a stricken land. The rich top-soil that formerly made the Champagne one of the fat provinces of France was gone, blown away and buried under by four years of incessant shell-fire. Areas that had been forested showed only blackened, branchless stumps, upthrust through the churned earth. What was left was naked, leprous chalk. It was a wilderness of craters, large and small, wherein no yard of earth lay untouched. Interminable mazes of trench work threaded this waste, discernible from a distance by the belts of rusty wire entanglements that stood before them. Of the great national highway that had once marched across the Champagne between rows of stately poplars, no vestige remained.

The second-in-command, peering from the pines with other officers of the battalion, could see nothing that moved in all the desolation. Men were there, thousands of them, but they were burrowed like animals in the earth. North of Somme-Py, even then, Gouraud's hard-fighting Frenchmen were blasting their way through the lines that led up to the last strongholds of the Boche toward Blanc Mont Ridge, and over this mangled terrain could be seen the smoke and fury of bursting shrapnel shell and high explosive. The sustained roar of artillery and the infernal clattering of machine-guns and musketry beat upon the ears of the watchers. Through glasses one could make out bits of blue and bits of green-gray, flung casually about between the trenches. These, the only touches of color in the waste, were the unburied bodies of French and German dead.

"So this, Slover, is the Champagne," said the second-in-command to one of his non-coms who stood beside him. The sergeant spat. "It looks like hell, sir!" he said.

The lieutenant strolled over to where a French staff captain stood with a knot of officers in the edge of the pines, pointing out features of this extended field, made memorable by bitter fighting.

"Since 1914 we have fought hard here," he was saying. "Oh, the French know this Champagne well, and the Boche knows it too. Yonder"—he pointed to the southwest—"is the Butte de Souain, where our Foreign Legion met in the first year that Guard Division that the Prussians call the 'Cockchafers.' They took the Butte, but most of the Legion are lying there now. And yonder"—the Frenchman extended his arm with a gesture that had something of the salute in it—"stands the Mountain of Rheims. If you look

—the air is clearing a little—you can perhaps see the towers of Rheims itself."

A long grayish hill lay against the gray sky at the horizon, and over it a good glass showed, very far and faint, the spires of the great cathedral, with a cloud of shell-fire hanging over them.

"All this terrain, as far as Rheims, is dominated by Blanc Mont Ridge yonder to the north. As long as the Boche holds Blanc Mont, he can throw his shells into Rheims; he can dominate the whole Champagne Sector, as far as the Marne. Indeed, they say that the Kaiser watched from Blanc Mont the battle that he launched here in July. And the Boche means to hang on there. So far, we have failed to dislodge him. I expect"—he broke off and smiled gravely on the circle of officers—"you will see some very hard fighting in the next few days, gentlemen!"

It was the last day of September, and as the forenoon went by an intermittent drizzle sent the battalion to such miserable shelters as the men could improvise. Company commanders and seconds-in-command went up toward ruined Somme-Py for reconnoissance, and returned to profane the prospect to their platoon leaders.

"I do not like this place," declared the captain of the 49th Company to his juniors. "It looks like it was just built for calamities to happen in."

"Yep, and all the division is around here for calamities to happen to. . . . A sight more of us will go in than will ever come out of it!"

Meantime it was wet and cold in the dripping shelters. Winter clothing had not been issued, and the battalion shivered and was not cheerful.

"Wish to God we could go up an' get this fight over with!"

"Yes, an' then go back somewhere for the winter. Let some of these here noble National Army outfits we've been hearin' about do some of the fightin'! There's us, and there's the 1st Division, and the 32nd—Hell! we ain't hogs! Let some of them other fellows have the glory——"

"Gawd help the Boche when we meets him this time! Somebody's got to pay for keepin' us out in this wet an' cold."

"Hear your young men talk, El Capitan? They're goin' to take it out on the Boche—they will, too. Don't you take any more of this than your rank entitles you to! I'm gettin' wet."

The second-in-command and the captain were huddled under a small sheet of corrugated iron, stolen by an enterprising orderly from the French gunners. The captain was very large, and the other very lean, and they were both about the same length. They fitted under the sheet by a sort of dovetailing process that made it complicated for either to move. A second-in-command is sort of an understudy to the company commander. In some of the outfits the captain does everything, and his understudy can only mope around and wait for his senior to become a casualty. In others, it is the junior who gets things done, and the captain is just a figurehead. In the 49th, however, the relation was at its happiest. The big captain and his lieutenant functioned together as smoothly as parts of a sweet-running engine, and there was between them the undemonstrative affection of men who have faced much peril together.

"As for me," rejoined the captain, drawing up one soaked knee and putting the other out in the wet, "I want to get wounded in this fight. A bon blighty, in the arm or the leg, I think. Something that will keep me in a nice dry hospital until spring. I don't like cold weather. Now who is pushin'? It's nothin' to me, John, if your side leaks—keep off o'mine!"

So the last day of September, 1918, passed, with the racket up forward unabated. So much of war is just lying around waiting in more or less discomfort. And herein lies

French grenadier—Blanc Mont.

the excellence of veterans. They swear and growl horribly
under discomfort and exposure—far more than green
troops; but privations do not sap their spirit or undermine
that intangible thing called morale. Rather do sufferings
nourish in the men a cold, mounting anger, that swells to
sullen ardor when at last the infantry comes to grips with
the enemy, and then it goes hard indeed with him who
stands in the way.

On the front, a few kilometres from where the battalion
lay and listened to the guns, Gouraud's attack was coming
to a head around the heights north of Somme-Py and the
strong trench systems that guarded the way to Blanc Mont
Ridge. Three magnificent French divisions, one of Chas-
seurs, a colonial division, and a line division with a Verdun
history, shattered themselves in fruitless attacks on the
Essen Trench and the Essen Hook, a switch line of that
system. Beyond the Essen line the Blanc Mont position
loomed impregnable. Late on the 1st of October, a gray,
bleak day, the battalion got its battle orders, and took over
a mangled front line from certain weary Frenchmen.

Gathering the platoon leaders and non-coms around
them, the captain and the second-in-command of the 49th
Company spread a large map on the ground, weighting its
corners with their pistols.

"You give the dope, John," ordered the captain, who was
not a man of words, and his junior spoke somewhat in this
manner:

"Here, you birds, look at this map. The Frogs have
driven the Boche a kilometre and a half north of Somme-
Py. You see it here—the town you watched them shell this
morning. They have gotten into the Prussian trench—this
blue line with the wire in front of it. It's just a fire trench,
mostly shell-holes linked up. Behind it, quite close, is the
Essen trench, which is evidently a hum-dinger! Concrete
pill-boxes and deep dugouts and all that sort of thing—
regular fort. The Frogs say it can't be taken from the front
—they've tried. We're goin' to take it. On the other side of

that is the Elbe trench, and a little to the left the Essen Hook, and in the centre the Bois de Vipre—same kind o' stuff, they say. We're to take them. You see them all on the map. . . . Next, away up in this corner of the map, is the Blanc Mont place. Whoever is left when we get that far will take that, too. . . . Questions? . . . Yes, Tom, we ought to get to use those sawed-off shotguns they gave us at St. Mihiel—though when we get past the Essen system, we'll be in the open, mostly. . . . The old Deuxième Division is goin' in to-night—it's goin' to be some party!"

"Gunnery sergeants send details from each platoon for bandoleers—ammunition dump is around Battalion Head-quarters somewhere," added the captain. "We get a few rifle-grenades, and some shotgun-shells. And make the men hang on to their reserve rations, for Christ's sake! Probably won't eat again until after this is over. Move out of here as soon as it's dark. That's all."

"Two hundred and thirty-four men, sir, and seven offi-cers, not counting the galley force and the office force that we're leaving behind," reported the second-in-command, falling in beside the captain as the company moved off with the rest of the battalion in the gathering darkness. They went in double file, dim shapes in the gloom, down the muddy, tortuous road.

"The company's in better shape than it ever has been," replied the captain thoughtfully. "St. Mihiel was a walk-over, but it was fine training for them, and even our green-est replacements had a chance to get over being gun-shy. And the noncoms are fine, too . . . hope we don't lose too many of them. You and I have come all the way from Belleau Wood together, John—I'm no calamity-howler—but there's something about this dam' Champagne country that gets you——"

"Too many men died here, I reckon," said the lieutenant. "You feel 'em somehow, in the dark. . . . Something creepy about those flares, isn't there?"

The road here was screened on the side toward the enemy

by coarse mats of camouflage material erected on tall poles. Through this screen the German flares, ceaselessly ascending, shone with cold, greenish whiteness, so that men saw their comrades' faces weirdly drawn and pale under their helmets. The files talked as they went——

"I've seen the time I'd have called those things pretty—but now—reckon hell's lit with the same kind of glims!" . . . "Remember the flare that went up in our faces the night we made the relief in Bellew Woods? Seemed to me like everybody in the world was lookin' at me." "Bois de Belleau! mighty few in the battalion now that remember them days, sonny. . . ." "Listen to that dam' Heine machine-gun over yonder . . . like a typewriter, ain't it?" "Useter run a typewriter myself, back befo' Texas declared war on Germany—in a nice dry office it was, an' this time o' night I'd be down on the drug-store corner lookin' 'em over.—" "Somebody shoot that bum, talkin' about lookin' 'em over!" "Hey! Th' angels'll be lookin him over, this time to-morrow night, they will!" "Yes, they will! I'll live to spit on the grave of the man that said that!"—"My word! Don't these 1917 model gyrines talk rough, Mac!" marvelled one old non-com to another.

The road passed into the desolation and wound north, kilometre after kilometre. Presently the camouflage ended and the battalion felt exceedingly naked without its shelter. Then a slope to the left screened the way, the crest of it sharply outlined as the flares ascended. Beyond that crest the machine-guns sounded very near; now and again the air was filled with the whispering rush of their bullets, passing high toward some chance target in the rear. The upper air was populous with shells passing, and the sky flickered with gun-flashes, but the road along which the battalion went enjoyed for the time an uneasy immunity. The rests were all too short; the sweating files swore at their heavy packs; the going was very hard. Presently the road ceased to be a road—merely a broken way across an interminable waste of shell-holes, made passable after a fashion by the hasty

Those sawed-off shotguns they gave us at St. Mihiel.

work of French engineers, toiling behind the assault of the infantry.

The battalion skirted stupendous craters of exploded mines—"Good Gawd! you could lose my daddy's house, an' his barn, too, in that there hole! 'Taint no small barn, either!" The stars had come out, and shone very far off and strangely calm. The dark was foul with all the reek of an old battle-field. "After mid-night," conjectured the files. "Are we ever goin' to get across this accursed place?"

The files plodded on each side of the tumbled track, and as they neared Somme-Py a pitiful stream of traffic grew and passed between them, the tide of French wounded ebbing to the rear. They were the débris of the attacks that had spent themselves through the day—walking wounded, drifting back like shadows in stained blue uniforms, men who staggered and leaned against each other and spoke in low, racked voices to the passing files; and broken men who were borne in stretchers, moaning—"Ah, Jesu! . . ." "Doucement, doucement!! . . ." Farther back the ambulances would be waiting for them. . . . The battalion went on in close-mouthed silence. Very little talking now, no laughing at all. . . . "El Capitan, regardez—we be sober-minded men approaching—what we approach—" said the second-in-command, hitching the sling of his musette bag well out of the way of his gas-mask. "I have always," replied that stolid veteran, "held that war was a serious business." . . . "This is Somme-Py. Can't those bums ahead set a better pace?"

The column went quickly through the town, into which shells were falling, stumbling over the débris of ruined walls and houses. There was a very busy French dressing-station there, under the relic of a church. It was too dark to see, but each man caught the sound and the smell of it. They cleared the town and went on to a crossroads. French guides were to have met the battalion there, for the line was just ahead, but the guides were late. There was a nerve-racking halt. The next battalion in column closed up; a machine-gun outfit, with its solemn, blasé mules, jammed into the rifle companies.

The 49th was the leading company, just behind the Battalion Headquarters group, and the second-in-command went up to where the major and his satellites were halted.

"Crossroads are always a dam' bad business, Coxy," the major was observing to his adjutant. "Just askin' for it here —no tellin' how late our Frog friends will be—get the men moved into that ditch off the road yonder—Ah! thought so!"

A high, swift whine that grew to a shrieking roar, and a five-inch shell crashed down some fifty yards to the right of the crowded road. Everybody except the mules were flat on the ground before it landed, but wicked splinters of steel sung across the road, and a machine-gunner, squatting by his cart, collapsed and rolled toward the edge of the road, swearing and clutching at his thigh. The men moved swiftly and without disorder to the ditch, which was a deep communication-trench paralleling the road. Another shell came as they moved, falling to the left, and then another, closer, this time between the road and the trench. A mule or two reared and plunged, stricken; a Marine whose head had been unduly high slumped silently down the side of the trench with most of his head gone. "Damn! Jimmie stopped somethin' the size of a stove-lid!" "Fool oughta kept his head down!" "Some very hard men you have in your company, El Capitan," commented the second-in-command, a few feet away, crouching by the side of the captain. "Now, I may stop one, but nobody's goin' to get to say that about me, I'll bet!" "Nor me, John!" ... "Face it when it comes, but no use lookin' for it!"

More shells came, landing along the road, between the road and the trench, and one or two of them in the trench itself. Cries and groans came from the head of the column; stretcher-bearers hurried in that direction; the battalion

lay close and waited. Then the shelling stopped. Up forward the major drew a long breath. "Just harassin' fire on
these crossroads. I was afraid we were spotted. Now, those
guides—" A little group of Frenchmen arrived panting at
the head of the column and the men were quickly on the
move again. "If Brother Boche had kept flingin' them sea-
bags around here, he'd a-hurt somebody. Where do we go
from here?"

Said the major, coming to the head of the 49th with a
French guide—"Francis, we're takin' the regimental front
—division's putting four battalions in the line. The 6th will
be on our left; infantry brigade on the right. Let me know
how your sector looks—my P.C. will be—I'd better send a
runner with you. Here's your guide."

That company moved off, and the other companies,
going into position in the battered Prussian trench, facing
the formidable Essen work. The French riflemen they
found there were hanging on in the very teeth of the
enemy. Their position had been hastily constructed a few
days before by the hard-pressed Boche and was a mere selection from the abundant shell craters, connected by shallow digging. The Marines stumbled and slipped through its
windings. It was cluttered up with dead men, for it had
been strongly held and dearly won. The 49th took over the
part allotted to it from some ten platoons of Frenchmen,
eight or ten men to a platoon, in command of a first lieutenant. It was what was left of a full battalion.

Courteous and suave, although he swayed on his feet
from weariness and his eyelids drooped from loss of sleep,
the Frenchman summed up the situation for the Marine
captain. "We hold this fire trench. In your sector are four
communication trenches running to the Essen work, which
is about a hundred metres distant. We hold most of the
boyau on the extreme right; the others we have barricaded.
You cannot take this Essen trench by frontal assault!"—
"Why can't we?" growled the American.

"When it is light you will see, M. le Capitaine! You can only get forward by bombing your way in the boyaux. They are too strong in machine-guns, the Boche. Now I take my men and go. Seven days and nights we have been on our feet . . . those of us who are left are very tired. . . .

The shells began to drop into the trench.

It is well that you be watchful in this place, but do not stir up the Boche yonder. They shoot with minenwerfers when you frighten them. Such a one finished my pauvre capitaine and six men with him. Bon chance, mon capitaine! Bon jour!"

"Cheerful bird, wasn't he?" remarked the captain.

"Wonder if that thing I stepped on just outside his hole was his captain? John, before it gets good daylight, don't you want to take a look-see at this Essen Trench? Take whoever you want and see how the land lies."

The Essen Trench had been very active when the companies were being posted; staccato bursts of machine-gun fire had ripped across the intervening dark, and Springfields had answered. There had been some bombing around traverses in the boyaux. But when, in the creeping grayness of the dawn, the lieutenant from the 49th ventured across to it with his orderly and a sergeant, he found the Boche retiring. Filing quickly through the communication trenches, the battalion occupied it without difficulty, and, looking around them, were very glad they hadn't had to take it by storm.

And the captain understood why the French lieutenant had said it couldn't be stormed. The French had tried the evening before to cross the scant distance and get into it. Most of those who had charged lay as the Boche Maxims had cut them down. In one place, between two boyaux that formed with the opposed lines a rough square of perhaps one hundred yards, he counted eighty-three dead Frenchmen. Lying very thick near the lip of their own trench, the bodies formed a sort of wedge, thinning toward the point as they had been decimated, and that point was one great bearded Frenchman, his body all a mass of bloody rags, who lay with his eyes fiercely open to the enemy and his outthrust bayonet almost in the emplacement where the Boche guns had been.

The company, which had learned its own bitter lesson in frontal attacks on machine-guns, gave passing tribute. "Them Frogs, they eat machine-guns up. Fightin' sons o' guns, they are. Wonder if any chow is comin' up to-day?" They made themselves comfortable among the dead and waited the next move with equanimity.

"Two hundred and thirty-one men, sir," reported the

A flare during shelling in the front-line trenches.

second-in-command, sliding into the shallow dugout where the captain was holed up. "Mighty lucky so far. I'm goin' to sleep. There's some shellin', especially toward the left, but most of the outfit is pretty well under cover."

II

Gouraud's battle roared on to the left with swelling tumult. The Americans, in their sector, passed the day in ominous quiet. They wondered what the delay was, speculated on the strategy of attack—which is a matter always sealed from the men who deliver the attack—and wore through to the evening of October 2. At dark, food came up in marmite cans—beef and potatoes and a little coffee. "Put ours on that mess-tin there," directed the second-in-command, as his orderly slid in with his and the captain's rations. The captain sat up in his corner a little later. "What th' hell, John?"—sniff—sniff! "Has that dead Boche on the other side of you begun to announce hisself? Phew!" The second-in-command rose from the letter he was writing by the stub of a candle and sniffed busily— sniff—snnnn—"Damnation! Captain, it's our supper!" With averted face he presented the grayish chunks of beef that reposed on the mess-tin. "Urggg—throw it out!" He disappeared up the crumbled steps to the entrance of the hole.

A few minutes later he slid down again, followed in a shower of dust and clods by a battalion runner. "All the beef was bad, El Capitan! What the young men are saying about the battalion supply would make your hair curl!— And here's our attack orders."

There was a brief pencilled order from the major, and maps. The two officers bent over them eagerly. "Runner!— Platoon commanders report right away—" . . . "What do you make of it, John? Looks like General Lejeune was goin' to split his division and reunite it on the field. . . . Hmmm! Ain't that the stunt you claim only Robert E. Lee and

In the Essen trench—a runner.

Napoleon could get away with? . . . All here? Get around—the map's about oriented——"

"Here we are, in the Essen Trench—seems that the Marines move down to the left to here—and the 9th and 23rd move to the right—to here. These pencil lines show the direction of attack—then we jump off, angling a little to the right, compass bearing—and the infantry outfits point about as much to the left. That brings us together up here about three kilometres, and we go on straight, a little west of north from there, to Blanc Mont——

"Essen Hook and Bois de Vipre are the first objectives—Blanc Mont final objective. . . . That means we pass to the flank of the Hook and join up behind the Viper Woods—we'll get some flanking fire, but we will cut both positions off from the rear, and we won't get near as many men shot up as we would in frontal attack. Might be worse——"

"That's all we know about the division orders—For the battalion, the major says the 5th Regiment will follow the 6th in support at the jump-off, and the zero hour will be communicated later—some time in the morning, I reckon. That's all."

The morning of October 3 [1918] came gray and misty. From midnight until dawn the front had been quiet at that point—comparatively. Then all the French and American guns opened with one world-shaking crash. From the Essen Trench the ground fell away gently, then rose in a long slope, along which could be made out the zigzags of the German trenches. The Bois de Vipre was a bluish mangled wood, two kilometres north. Peering from their shelters, the battalion saw all this ground swept by a hurricane of shell-fire. Red and green flames broke in orderly rows where the 75s showered down on the Boche lines; great black clouds leaped up where the larger shells fell roaring. The hillside and the wood were all veiled in low-hanging smoke, and the flashes came redly through the cloud. Far off, Blanc

Mont way, a lucky shell found and exploded a great am-munition-dump—the battalion felt the long tremor from the shock of it come to them through the earth and watched, minutes after the high crimson flare of the explo-sion, a broad column of smoke that shot straight up from it, hundreds of feet, and hung in air, spreading out at the top like some unearthly tree.

The men crowed and chortled in the trench. "Boy, ain't Heinie gettin' it now!" "Hear that shell gurglin' as she goes?—That's gas." "Listen to them 75s. You know, I never see one of them little guns that I don't want to go up and kiss it. Remember that counter-attack they smeared in front of us at Soissons?"

The heavens seemed roofed over with long, keening noises—sounds like the sharp ripping of silk, magnified, running in swift arcs from horizon to horizon. These were the quickfiring 75s, the clear-cut bark of the discharges merging into a crashing roar. Other sounds came with them, deeper in key, the whine growing to a rumble—these were the heavier shells—105s, 155s, 210s. Almost, one ex-pected to look up and see them, like swift, deadly birds, some small, some enormous, all terrible. Gas-shells could be distinguished from the high explosive by the throaty gurgle of the liquid in them. "Move down the trench to the left," came the order.

The battalion moved, filing around the traverses with judicious intervals between men, so that the Boche shells might not include too many in their radius of death. For Heinie was beginning to shoot back. He had the range of his vacated trench perfectly, and, holding the high ground, he could see what he was shooting at. Shells began to crash down among the companies, whole squads were blotted out, and men choked and coughed as the reek of the high explo-sive caught at their windpipes.

"Lordy, ain't we ever goin' to get outa this dam' place an' get at 'em—?" A shell with a driving-band loose came with

The morning of October 3d came gray and misty—a patrol.

a banshee scream, and men and pieces of men were blown into the air. "That was in the first platoon," said the second-in-command, shaking the dirt off his gas-mask. "Something ought to be done about that gunner, El Capitan!" Another landed in the opposite lip of the trench where the two officers crouched, half-burying them both. "My God, cap'n! You killed?" "Hell, no! Are you?"

"Far enough to the left," the major sent word. "We will

"Lordy, ain't we ever goin' to get outa this dam' place an get at 'em—?"

wait here. The 6th leads—we're the last battalion in support to-day."

Coming from the maze of trenches in the rear, the assault regiment began to pass through the 5th, battalion following battalion at 500-yard distances. A number of French "baby" tanks started with the assaulting waves, but it was an evil place for tanks. Tank traps, trenches so wide that the little fellows went nose-down into them and stuck, and direct fire from Boche artillery stopped the most of them. Wave after wave, the 6th went forward. For a moment the sun shone through the murk, near the horizon —a smouldering red sun, banded like Saturn, and all the bayonets gleamed like blood. Then the cloud closed again.

When an attack is well launched it is the strategy of the defenders to concentrate their artillery fire on the support waves that follow the assault troops, leaving the latter to be dealt with by machine-gun and rifle fire. So the battalion, following on in its turn, was not happy.

"Wish to Gawd we wuz up forward," growled the files. " 'Nothin' up there but machine-guns. This here shellin' gets a man's goat. Them bums in the 6th allus did have all the luck! . . ." "Lootenant, ain't we ever gonna get a chance at them Boches? This bein' killed without a chance to kill back is hell—that's what it is!"

The battalion was out of the trench now, and going forward, regulating its pace on the battalion ahead. All at once there was a snapping and crackling in the air—a corporal spun round and collapsed limply, while his blouse turned red under his gas-mask—the man beside him stumbled and went down, swearing through grayish lips at a shattered knee—the men flattened and all faces turned toward the flank.

"Machine-guns on the left!"—"Hell! It's that Essen Hook we've got to pass—thank God, it's long range! Come on, you birds." And the battalion went on, enduring grimly. Finally, when well past its front, which ran diagonally to the line of advance, the 17th Company, that had the left, turned savagely on the Essen Hook and got a foothold in its rear. A one-pounder from the regimental headquarters company was rushed up to assist them, and the men yelled with delight as the vicious little cannon got in direct hits on the Boche emplacements. Hopelessly cut off, the large body of Germans in this formidable work surrendered after a few sharp and bloody minutes, and the 17th, sending back its prisoners, rejoined the battalion.

Prisoners began to stream back from the front of the attack, telling of the success of the 6th. Wounded came with them, some walking, some carried on improvised stretchers by the Boche "kamarads." Most of them were grinning. "Goin' fine up there, boys, goin' fine!" "Lookit, fellers! Got a bon blighty—We'll give 'em your regards in Paris!"

Others of the 6th lay on the ground over which the battalion passed. Some lay quietly, like men who rested after labor. Others were mangled and twisted into attitudes grotesque and horrible as the fury of the exploding shells had flung them. There were dead Germans, too. Up forward

Others lay on the ground over which the battalion passed.

rifle-fire and machine-guns gave tongue, and all the Boche guns raged together. "Reckon the 6th is gettin' to Blanc Mont now." The second-in-command looked at his watch. Inconceivably, it was noon.

For a while now the battalion halted, keeping its distance from the unit ahead. The men lay on their rifles and expressed unreasonable yearnings for food. "Eat? Eat? Hell! Shock troops ain't supposed to eat!" Officers cast anxious glances toward the utterly exposed left. The French attack had failed to keep abreast of the American.

The left company, the 17th, was in a cover of scrubby
trees. The other companies were likewise concealed. Only
the 49th lay perforce in the open, on a bleak, shell-pocked
slope. A high-flying Boche plane spotted its platoon columns, asprawl eighty or a hundred yards apart on the
chalky ground. "No good," said the second-in-command,
cocking his head gander-wise in his flat helmet, "is goin' to
come of that dam' thing—guess all our noble aviators have
gone home to lunch." The plane, high and small and shining
in the sky, circled slowly above them. Far back of the
Boche lines there was a railroad gun that took a wireless
from the wheeling vulture. "Listen," said the captain,
"listen to th——"

There were lots of shells passing over—the long, tearing
whine of the 75s, the coarser voices of the Boche 77s replying, and heavy stuff, but most of it was breaking behind or
in front of the battalion. Into this roof of sound came a
deeper note—a far-off rumble that mounted to an enormous shattering roar, like a freight train on a down-grade.
The company flattened against the ground like partridges,
and the world shook and reeled under them as a nine-inch
shell crashed into the earth fifty yards ahead, exploding
with a cataclysmic detonation that rocked their senses. An
appalling geyser of black smoke and torn earth leaped sky-
ward, jagged splinters of steel whined away, and stones and
clods showered down. Before the smoke had lifted from the
monstrous crater the devastating rumble came again, and
the second shell roared down fifty yards to the rear.

"Oh, Lordy! They've got us bracketed!"

"I saw that one! I saw it—look right where the next one's
gonna hit, an'—" "Look where it's gonna hit! Lawd, if I
jest knew it wasn't gonna hit me—ahh——!"

The third shell came, and men who risked an eye could
see it—a dark, tremendous streak, shooting straight down
to the quivering earth. A yawning hole opened and thunder fairly between two platoon columns, and the earth

"Oh Lordy! They've got us bracketed!"

vomited. . . . It was wonderful shooting. All the shells that followed dropped between the columns of prone men—but not a man was hit! The heavy projectiles sank far into the chalky soil, and the explosions sent the deadly fragments outward and over the company. More than a dozen shells were fired in all, the high sinister plane wheeling overhead the while. Then the company went forward with the battalion, very glad to move.

"Any one of those nine-inch babies would have blotted out twenty of us," marvelled a lieutenant, leading his platoon around a thirty-foot crater that still smoked. "Or ripped the heart out of any concrete-and-steel fortification ever built—the good Lawd was certainly with us!"

To the company commanders, gathered at dark in a much disfigured Boche shelter in the Wood of Somme-Py, the major gave information. "The 6th took Blanc Mont, and they are holding it against heavy counter-attacks. Prisoners say they were ordered to hold here at any costs—they're fighting damned well, too! The infantry regiments piped down the Bois de Vipre, just as we did the Essen Hook. The division is grouping around the Ridge, but we're pretty well isolated from the French. Tonight we are going on up and take the front line, and attack toward St.-Etienne-à-Arnes—town north of the Ridge and a little west. Get on up to Blanc Mont with your companies—P. C. will be there, along the road that runs across the Ridge."

III

Not greatly troubled by the Boche shelling, that died to spasmodic bursts as the night went on, the battalion mounted through the dark to its appointed place. Here, beside a blasted road that ran along Blanc Mont, just behind the thin line of the 6th, the weary men lay down, and, no orders being immediately forthcoming, slept like the dead that were lying thickly there. Let the officers worry over

Before zero hour.

the fact that the French had fallen behind on each flank, that the division was, to all purposes, isolated far out in Boche territory—let any fool worry over the chances of stopping one to-morrow—to-morrow would come soon enough. "The lootenant says to get all the rest you can—don-t—nobody need to—tell—me—tha——"

In the deep dugouts behind the road the battalion commanders prodded at field-maps and swore wearily over the ominous gaps behind the flanks—three kilometres on one flank, five on the other, where the French divisions had not kept pace. Into these holes the Boche had all day been savagely striving to thrust himself, and his success would mean disaster. Already the 6th had a force thrown back to cover the left rear, disposed at right angles to the line of advance. . . . And orders were to carry the attack forward at dawn. On top of that, after midnight a Boche deserter crawled into the line with the cheering news that the Germans were planning an attack in force on the American flanks at dawn; a division of fresh troops—Prussians—had just been brought up for that purpose. It looked bad—it looked worse than that. "Well," said Major George Hamilton of the 1st Battalion of the 5th, "orders are to attack, and, by God, we'll attack"—a yawn spoiled the dramatic effect of his pronouncement—"and now I'm going to get some sleep. Coxy, wake me at 5:30—that will be an hour."

And at dawn, while the Ridge shook and thundered under the barrage that went before the Boche flank attack, and the 6th held with their rifles the branch behind the left, the 5th Marines went forward to carry the battle to St.-Etienne.

They went in column of battalions, four companies abreast. For the 1st Battalion, still in support, the fourth day of October began as a weary repetition of the day before. Shells whooped down into the platoon columns as they waited for the 2nd and 3d Battalions to get clear; machine-guns on the left took toll as they rose up to follow. Noon found them well forward of the Ridge, lying in an open flat, while the leading battalions disappeared in pine woods on a long slope ahead. It had fallen strangely quiet where they lay.

"Now what's comin', I wonder?" "Anything at all, 'cept chow." "Boy, ain't it quiet here? What do you reckon—" "Don't like this," said one old non-com to another. "Minds me of once when I was on a battle-wagon in the China Sea. Got still like this, and then all at once all the wind God ever let loose come down on us!" "Shouldn't wonder—Hey! She's opening up again! That there 2d Battalion has sure stuck its foot in somethin'!"

Up forward all hell broke loose. Artillery, machine-guns, rifles, even the coughing detonations of grenades, mounted to an inconceivable fury of sound. "Here comes a battalion runner—there's the skipper, over there—what's up, anyway?"

The second-in-command came through his company with a light in his eyes, and he sent his voice before him. "Deploy the first platoon, Mr. Langford. Three-pace interval, be sure. Where's Mr. Connor? Oh, Chuck, you'll form the second wave behind Tom. About fifty yards. Other two platoons in column behind the company flanks. On yo' feet, chillun! We're goin' up against 'em!"

And so, all four companies in line, the 1st Battalion, a thousand men, went up against the Boche. "Capitan," said the second-in-command, as they started, "we're swingin' half-left. This tack will take us right to St.-Etienne, won't it? We were pointin' a little one side of it before—major give you any dope?" "The Boche have come out of St.-Etienne—two full infantry regiments, anyhow, and a bunch of Maxim guns—and hit the second and third in the flank. Must be pretty bad. We're goin' up to hit them in the flank ourselves. 'Bout a kilometre, I'd say. Wait until

Flanking fire. "Hey! She's opening up again."

their artillery spots this little promenade. None of ours in support, you know."

The hush still hung around them as they moved out of the flat and began to ascend the long gray slope ahead, the crest of which was covered with a growth of pines. There was no cover on the slope—a few shell-holes, a few

The hush still hung around them as they moved out of the flat and began to ascend the long gray slope ahead.

stunted bushes and sparse tufts of grass. Across a valley to the left, 800 to 1,000 yards away, rose another ridge, thickly clothed with underbrush, that ran back toward Blanc Mont. Forward and to the right was the heavy pine timber into which the other battalions had gone, and from which still came tumult and clangor. Tumult and clangor, also, back toward Blanc Mont, and further back, where the French attacks were pushing forward, and

drumming thunder on the right, where the Saxons were
breaking against the 9th and 23d Infantry—but here,
quiet. Voices of non-coms, rasping out admonitions to the
files, sounded little and thin along the line. Every man
knew, without words, that the case was desperate, but to
this end was all their strength and skill in war, all their
cunning gained in other battles, and their hearts lifted up
to meet what might come. "More interval—more interval
there on the left! Don't bunch up, you————"

"That ridge over yonder, capitan—" said the second-in-
command softly. "It's lousy with the old Boche! And forward—and behind the flank, too! This is goin' to be—Ahhh
—shrapnel!"

The first shell came screaming down the line from the
right, and broke with the hollow cough and poisonous yellow puff of smoke which marks the particular abomination
of the foot-soldier. It broke fairly over the centre of the
49th, and every head ducked in unison. Three men there
were who seemed to throw themselves prone; they did not
get up again. And then the fight closed upon the battalion
with the complete and horrid unreality of nightmare. All
along the extended line the saffron shrapnel flowered, fling-
ing death and mutilation down. Singing balls and jagged
bits of steel spattered on the hard ground like sheets of hail;
the line writhed and staggered, steadied and went on, clos-
ing toward the centre as the shells bit into it. High-explo-
sive shells came with the shrapnel, and where they fell
geysers of torn earth and black smoke roared up to mingle
with the devilish yellow in the air. A foul murky cloud of
dust and smoke formed and went with the thinning companies, a cloud lit with red flashes and full of howling death.

The silent ridge to the left awoke with machine-guns
and rifles, and sibilant rushing flights of nickel-coated mis-
siles from Maxim and Mauser struck down where the shells
spared. An increasing trail of crumpled brown figures lay

The first shell came screaming down the line from the right.

behind the battalion as it went. The raw smell of blood was in men's nostrils.

Going forward with his men, a little dazed perhaps with shock and sound such as never were on earth before, the second-in-command was conscious of a strangely mounting sense of the unreality of the whole thing. Automatically functioning, as a company officer must, in the things he is trained to do, there was still a corner of his brain that watched detached and aloof as the scene unrolled. There was an officer rapped across the toe of his boot by a spent bullet—the leather wasn't even scratched—who sat down and asserted that his foot was shot off. There was Lieutenant Connor, who took a scrapnel dud in his loins, and was opened horribly. . . .

There was a sergeant, a hard old non-com of many battles, who went forward beside him. His face was very red, and his eyes were very bright, and his lean jaw bulged with a great chew of tobacco. His big shoulders were hunched forward, and his bayonet glinted at a thirsty angle, and his sturdy putteed legs swung in an irresistible stride. Then there was, oddly audible through the din, the unmistakable sound that a bullet makes when it strikes human flesh—and a long, crumpled, formless thing on the ground turned to the sky blind eyes in a crawling mask of red. There were five men with a machine-gun, barrel and mount and ammunition-boxes, and a girlish, pink-cheeked lieutenant went before them swinging a pair of field-glasses in his hand. Over and a little short of them a red sun flashed in a whorl of yellow smoke, and they were flattened into a mess of bloody rags, from which an arm thrust upward, dangling a pair of new, clean glasses by a thong, and remained so. . . . The woods on the crest were as far away as ever through the murk—their strides got them nowhere—their legs were clogged as in an evil dream—they were falling so fast, these men he had worked with and helped to train in war. There was a monstrous anger in his heart . . . a five-

"Here comes a battalion runner—what's up, anyway?"

inch shell swooped over his head, so near that the rush of air made his ear-drums pop and burst. He was picked up and whirled away like a leaf, breath and senses struck from him by the world-shattering concussion.

The second-in-command was pulled to his feet by Gunner Nice, who had taken the second platoon. His head lolled stupidly a moment, then he heard words—"an' that shell got all the captain's group, sir—all of 'em! An' my platoon's all casualties—" He pulled himself together as he went forward. His raincoat was split up the back, under his belt. His map-case was gone—the strap that had secured it hung loosely from his shoulder. There was blood on his hands, and the salt taste of it in his mouth, but it didn't seem to be his. And the front of the battalion was very narrow, now. The support platoons were all in the line. Strangest of all, the gray slope was behind them—the trees on the crest were only a few yards away.

Behind and to the left the machine-guns still raved, but the artillery fell away. A greenish rocket flared from the pines ahead, and right in the faces of the panting Marines machine-guns and rifles blazed. In the shadow of the pines were men in cumbersome green-gray uniforms, with faces that looked hardly human under deep round helmets. With eyes narrowed, bodies slanting forward like men in heavy rain, the remnant of the battalion went to them.

It was the flank of the Boche column which had come out of St.-Etienne and struck the leading battalions of the 5th. It had watched first with keen delight, then with incredulity, the tortured advance of the battalion. It had waited too long to open its own fire. And now, already shaken by the sight of these men who would not die, it shrank from the long American bayonets and the pitiless, furious faces behind the steel. A few Brandenburger zealots elected to die on their spitting Maxim guns, working them until bayonets or clubbed rifles made an end. A few iron-souled Prussians—the Boche had such men—stood up to meet bayonet with bayonet, and died that way. The second-in-command saw such a one, a big feldwebel, spring against one of his sergeants with the long Prussian lunge that throws the bayonet like a spear to the full reach of the arm. It is a spectacular thrust, and will split like a rabbit what stands in its way. But the sergeant, Bob Slover, a little fiery man with a penchant for killing Germans, ran under it and thrust from the ground for the Boche's throat. And as his point touched, he pulled the trigger. The feldwebel's helmet flew straight into the air, and the top of his head went with it.

A great many more flung away their arms and bleated "Kamaraden" to men who in that red minute knew no mercy. Some hid in holes, or feigned death, to be hunted out as the press thinned. And the rest scuttled through the fringe of trees and back down toward St.-Etienne, while the Marines, lying prone or taking rest for their Springfields, killed them as they ran. This same rifle-fire, directed against the flank and rear of the column which had pushed to the right against the other battalions of the 5th, broke that force and dispersed it. There was a battery of field-guns down the slope, 500 yards or so. The gunners—those who were lucky—took to cover after the first burst of fire. "Thank Gawd fer a shot at them dam' artillerymen! Battle-sight, an' aim low, you birds—don't let any of them bastards get away!" . . . "Sergeant, reckon the lootenant would let us go down an' take them 77s?—"Shut up an' work yo' bolt, you dam' fool!—Whatinell you think you are—a army core?"—"Besides, Mr. Connor's dead. . . ." On the hill beyond St.-Etienne new trenches scarred the slope; there were many Germans milling there, some 1,500 yards away. "Save your ammunition and lay low," the word was passed. "We're on our own out here." And the battalion, a very small battalion now, little more than a hundred men, lay along the crest they had stormed, with their dead and wounded and the Boche dead and wounded around them.

A few iron-souled Prussians—the Boche had such men—stood up to meet bayonet with bayonet, and died that way.

Almost immediately the Boche began to react. He opened on them a storm of fire, high explosive and shrapnel, and his machine-guns dinned fiercely. A counter-attack began to form toward St.-Etienne. Sweating gunners struggled into position with the two machine-guns that were left in

The last few men are always the most difficult to kill.

the battalion, and these, with their crews, were knocked out by shell-fire before either had been in action long enough to fire a clip. But the rifles gave tongue and continued to speak—the last few men are always the most difficult to kill—and the Boche had little taste for rifle-fire that begins to kill at 700 yards. That counter-attack shortly returned whence it came, and the one that followed it went back also.

The rifles fell silent, for the Boche infantry was in cover, or too far away to waste scant ammunition on. "O Lord, for one battery of 75s or a machine-gun outfit! All the Boches in the world, an' nothin' to reach 'em with!" lamented the captain of the 49th. "We're clean away from our guns, and those devils seem to know it—look at 'em, yonder! Heard a shell from ours to-day, John? I haven't." —"Plenty from the other side, though—damn few of us left, capitan. Eastin's got it, Tom Langford's got it— Chuck Connor, and Matthews. Don't know where Geer is. Guess I'm the only officer you have left—here's Captain Whitehead."

Whitehead, of the 67th Company, plumped down beside them. Small, very quick and wiry, with his helmet cocked on the side of his head, he gave the impression of a fierce and warlike little hawk. "Hunt's comin' over, Francis," he said. "Bad place; worst I ever saw. Got about thirty men left. Hell that our machine-guns got knocked out so quick, wasn't it?—must be two regiments of Fritzies on our front yonder!"

Captain Hunt, senior in the field, a big, imperturbable Californian, came, and Lieutenant Kelly, promoted by casualties in the last hour to command of the 66th Company. "How does it look to you, gentlemen?" said Hunt. "Damn bad" was the consensus of opinion, with profane embellishments. Followed some technical discussion. "Well," concluded the senior captain, "we've accomplished our mission —broke up their attack—better hook up with the rest of the regiment. We'll find them through the woods to the right. Move off your companies—Kelly, you go first."

Nobody remembers very clearly that swing to the right, through a hail of machine-gun fire and an inferno of shelling. They found the companies of the 2nd Battalion digging in astride a blasted road, and went into position beside them.

"I've organized the company sector with twenty men— all we've got left—you and I make twenty-two," reported the second-in-command, dropping wearily into the shell-hole where the captain had established himself. "Lord, I'm tired . . . and what I can't see," he added in some wonder, fingering the rents in his raincoat, "is why we weren't killed too. . . ."

A machine-gunner, Champagne.
A sketch made on the field.

That night, lying in its shallow, hastily dug holes, the remnant of the battalion descended through further hells of shelling. The next night tins of beef and bread came up. There was some grim laughter when it came. "Captain," reported the one remaining sergeant, after distributing rations in the dark, "they sent us chow according to the last strength report—three days ago—230-odd rations. The men are building breastworks out of the corned-willy cans, sir!—twenty of 'em——"

Some runners got through, and Division H. Q., well forward in a pleasantly exposed spot on the Souain road, built up a picture of a situation sufficiently interesting. Four infantry regiments were thrust saw-wise northwest to northeast of Blanc Mont; all were isolated from each other and from the French, who had lagged behind the flanks. Four little islands in a turbulent Boche sea, and the old Boche doing his damnedest. The Marine major-general commanding, Lejeune, it is related, went serenely to sleep. And they relate further that a staff colonel who, like Martha, was careful and troubled about many things, came to rouse him with a tale of disaster: "General, general, I have word from the front that a regiment of Marines is entirely surrounded by the Germans!"

"Yes, colonel? Well, sir," said the general, sadly and sleepily, "I am sorry for those Germans!"—and returned to his slumbers.

More days and nights, slipping, characterless, into each other. Being less than a company in strength, the 1st Battalion of the 5th was not called on to attack again. They lay in their holes and endured. "Until the division has accomplished its mission," said the second-in-command, rubbing his dirt-encrusted and unshaven chin. "That means, until the rest of the outfit is killed down as close as we are. Then we'll be relieved, an' get a week's rest and a gang of bloodthirsty replacements, an' then we can do it all over again." "Yes," replied the captain, turning uneasily in the cramped, coffin-shaped hole in which they lay. He scratched himself. "I have cooties, I think. In plural quantities." "Well, you would have that orderly strip the overcoats off a covey of dead Boches to furnish this château of ours. The Boche is such an uncleanly beast. . . . I have cooties, too, my capitan. Hell . . . ain't war wonderful!"

And after certain days, the division was relieved. The battalion marched out at night. The drumming thunder of the guns fell behind them and no man turned his face to look again on the baleful lights of the front. On the road they passed a regiment of the relieving division—full, strong companies of National Guardsmen. They went up one side of the road; and in ragged column of twos, unsightly even in the dim and fitful light, the Marines plodded down the other side. They were utterly weary, with shuffling feet and hanging heads. The division had just done something that those old masters in the art of war, the French, and the world after them, including Ludendorff, were to acknowledge remarkable. They had hurled the Boche from Blanc Mont and freed the sacred city of Rheims. They had paid a price hideous even for this war. And they were spent. If there was any idea in those hanging heads it was food and rest.

The Guard companies gibed at the shrunken battalion as they passed. Singing and joking they went. High words of courage were on their lips and nervous laughter. Save for a weary random curse here and there, the battalion did not answer. . . . "Hell, them birds don't know no better. . . ." "Yeh, we went up singin' too, once—good Lord, how long ago! . . . They won't sing when they come out . . . or any time after . . . in this war." . . . "Damn you, can't you march on your own side the road? How much room you need?"

SONGS

THREE

"MADEMOISELLE FROM ARMENTIERES"

It was nice, back in billets, resting between battles, to sit on a bench in the sun and watch the world go by. Odette, the strapping and genteel daughter of the baker of Croutte-sur-Marne, here herds the duck Anatole into the courtyard of her mother's bakery. (M. Boulanger was last heard from on the Chemin des Dames; Mme. Boulangère keeps the establishment going.) The duck Anatole has been ordered for dinner by two lieutenants of the 1st Battalion, the consideration being 37 francs 80 centimes. Two privates of the 49th Company are choiring softly "Mademoiselle from Armentières" as she passes. It is just as well that neither Odette nor Anatole comprend l'anglais.

MONKEY-MEAT

At various times and places in 1918 the 2nd Marine Division was subsisted on the French ration, a component part of which was preserved Argentine beef with carrots in it. This was called monkey-meat by the Marines of the 4th Brigade. Men ate it when they were very hungry.

IN A MANGLED place called the Wood Northwest of Lucy-le-Bocage two lieutenants of the Marine Brigade squatted by a hole the size of a coffin and regarded with attention certain cooking operations. The older, and perhaps the dirtier of the two, was intent upon a fire-blackened mess-kit, which was balanced on two stones and two German bayonets over a can of solidified alcohol. In the mess-kit was simmering a grayish and unattractive matter with doubtful yellowish lumps, into which the lieutenant fed, discriminatingly, bits of hard bread and frayed tomatoes from a can.

"Do what you will with it," he observed, "monkey-meat is monkey-meat. It's a great pity that damn Tompkins had to get himself bumped off last night when we came out. He had a way with monkey-meat, the kid did—hell! I never have any luck with orderlies!" He prodded the mess of Argentine beef—the French army's canned meat ration—and stared sombrely. His eyes, a little bloodshot in his sunburnt, unshaven face, were sleepy.

The other waited on two canteen cups stilted precariously over a pale-lavender flame. The water in them began to boil, and he supplied coffee—the coarse-ground, pale coffee of the Frogs—with a spoon that shook a little. He considered: "S'pose I'd better boil the sugar in with it," he decided. "There isn't so much of it, you know. We'll taste it more." And he added the contents of a little muslin sack —heavy beet-sugar that looked like sand. His face was pale and somewhat troubled, and his week's beard was straggling and unwholesome. He was not an out-of-doors man

—and he was battalion scout officer. A gentleman over-sensitive for the rude business of war, he would continue to function until he broke—and one sensed that he would suffer while about it. . . .

"I don't like monkey-meat. Before this smell"—he waved his spoon petulantly—"got into my nose I never could eat it. But now you can't smell but one thing, and, after all, you've got to eat."

The smell he referred to lay through the wood like a tangible fog that one could feel against the cheek and see. It was the nub-end of June, and many battalions of fighting men had lain in the Wood Northwest of Lucy, going up to the front a little way forward or coming out to stand by in support. It was a lovely place for supports; you could gather here and debouch toward any part of the sector, from Hill 142, on the left, through the Bois de Belleau and Bouresches, to Vaux, where the infantry brigade took on. Many men had lain in the wood, and many men lay in it still. Some of these were buried very casually. Others, in hidden tangles of it, along its approaches, and in the trampled areas beyond it where attack and counter-attack had broken for nearly a month of days and nights, hadn't been buried at all. And always there were more, and the June sun grew hotter as it made toward July.

Troops lay in the wood now; a battalion of the 6th and two companies of the 5th Regiment outfit, half of which was still in line on the flank of the Bois de Belleau. These companies had come out at dawn, attended by shell-fire; they had plunged into the wood and slept where they halted, unawakened—except the wounded—by the methodical shelling to which the Boche treated the place every day. Now, in the evening, they were awake and hungry. They squatted, each man in his hole, and did what they could about it. A savage-looking lot, in battered helmets and dirty uniforms. But you saw them cleaning their rifles. . . .

"Hey, yuh dog-robbin' battalion runner, you—what's up!"

The scout officer, with his hand out to lift away the coffee, which was, in his judgment, boiled, heard: "Mr. Braxton? Yeh, he's up thataway, with the lootenant." "Hey, yuh dog-robbin' battalion runner, you—what's up? Hey?" "Scout officer? Over yonder, him wit' the green blouse—" and a soiled battalion runner, identified by his red brassard and his air of one laden with vital information, clumped up and saluted sketchily.

"Sir, the major wants to see the battalion scout officer at battalion headquarters. The major said: Right away, sir."

The scout officer swore, inexpertly, for he was not a profane fellow, but with infinite feeling. "Good God, I hope it ain't—If you can keep my coffee hot, Tommie— Be right back as soon as I can. Save my slum. Don't let anything happen to my slum—" The words trailed in the air as he went swiftly off, buckling his pistol-belt. The battalion commander was that kind of an officer.

The lieutenant growled in sympathy: "Somebody's always takin' the joy out of life. Jim, he's hungry as I am, an' that's as hungry as a bitch wolf. That's the trouble with this war stuff; man misses too many meals." He took the cooking from the fire and replaced the lids on the little alcohol cans with care. Canned heat was quite hard to come by; the Boche was much better provided with it; he was indebted for this to a deceased German gentleman, and it was the last he had.

"No tellin' what the old man wants. Glad I ain't a scout officer. This war's hard on Jim—he takes it too serious. I'll wait, though." Absently he drank the tomato juice left in the can. He tried his coffee, and burned his mouth. "Wish I had the man here that invented this aluminum canteen cup! Time the damn cup's cool enough so you won't burn the hide off yo' lip, the coffee's stone cold." Then, later: Not boiled enough. Jim, he's used to bein' waited on—never make a rustler, he won't. . . .

"He takes the war too serious."

"Well, he's long in comin'. Old man sent him forward to make a map or something, most prob'ly." He tasted the slum. "That Tompkins! Why the hell he had to stop one— only man I ever knew that could make this monkey-meat taste like anything! And he goes and gets bumped off. Hell! That's the way with these kids. This needs an onion."

He ate half the mess, with scrupulous exactness, and drank his coffee. He put the lid on the mess-kit, and covered Jim's coffee, now getting cold. He smoked a cigarette and talked shop with his platoon sergeant. He gave some very hard words and his last candle-end to a pale private who admitted blistered heels, and then stood over the man while he tallowed his noisome socks. He interviewed his chaut-chaut gunners, and sent them off to beg new clips from the battalion quartermaster sergeant. It grew into the long French twilight; Boche planes were about, and all the anti-aircraft stuff in the neighborhood was furiously in action. Strolling back to his hole, the lieutenant observed that the pale private had resumed his shoes and was rolling his puttees with a relieved look. At this moment the nose-cap of a 75 came whimpering and hirpling down out of the heavens and gutted the fellow. . . . When that was cleaned up, the lieutenant lay in his hole, weighing the half-empty mess-kit in his hands, and trusted that nothing unseemly had happened to Jim. He thought of going up to battalion to see what was doing—but the major liked for you to stay with your men, unless he sent for you. . . . "Well! Might as well get some sleep. . . ."

Toward dark the Boche began to slam 77s and 150s into the Wood northwest of Lucy. It became a place of horror, with stark cries in the night, between the rending crashes of the shells. About an hour before midnight the word was passed and the two companies got out and went up across the pestilential wheat-fields and into the Bois de Belleau.

That same afternoon an unassigned colonel had come up

to Brigade Headquarters. Wanted to go to Paris, he did, and the brigade commander said that the only way to get there was to bring in a prisoner. One prisoner; seven days' leave. Be glad to get a prisoner. Intelligence had word of a new division or so moved in over there last night; identification not yet positive.

This colonel took steps. He was a man of parts and very desirous of the fleshpots of the Place de l'Opéra. There was an elegant French captain attached to brigade for no very evident reason—just attached—spoke English and knew vintages. Said to be an expert on raids. The colonel put it up to him in such and such a way: would he go? Yes, but certainly. Just a small raid, my colonel? Oh, a very small raid. Now, as to artillery support—a map was broken out.

Brigade artillery officer—chap the colonel knew out on the Asiatic station—happened in. How about it—just about half as much stuff as you fellows wasted on the Tartar Wall that time—eh? Sure: it could be arranged. Ten minutes' intensive; say, one battery; where you want it? Brigade intelligence took thought: They've got some kind of a strong point out from the ruined airdrome in front of Torcy. Their line is through Torcy; battalion in there. Left of the Bois—see here? Our photos show two big craters— some of the heavy stuff they shot at the railroad the 29th of May, or the 30th, most likely—eh, m'sieur le capitaine? Might look at that, colonel. Best jump-off is from Terry's battalion—about here—he has two companies here. Six hundred yards to go; keep the Bois well away—well starboard, as you leathernecks say; come back the same route. Wheat. Little gully here. Craters just beyond. Main line at least a hundred metres back. Good? Let's call up Terry and see if he'll give you the men. . . . Terry would give him twenty-five men and two chaut-chauts and not a Marine more. Who wanted a raid, anyway? Sending two support companies up to the Bois as soon as it's dark. Looks interestin' on the right. . . . Good! All set. Start your covering fire at 23

hours 15. You jump off at 23 hours 19. Take you six minutes to get over, huh? "All right, colonel, bonne chance!"

Just before dark the colonel and Captain de Stegur were
at battalion headquarters. "Whitehead will give you your
men, and I'm sending my scout officer along. Needs that
sort of thing. Be sure you come back where you went out.
Crabbe's to the right of there. You know Crabbe. Shoots
quick."

"But, my colonel," represented Captain de Stegur, "one
should arrange, one should explain, one should instruct—in
effect, one should rehearse——"

"Rehearse hell, sir! I'm due in Paris to-morrow night.
Where those Marines, major? I'll tell 'em what I want——"

So it was that a wedge of men debouched into the wheat
at 23 hours 19 minutes;* it being sufficiently dark.

The battalion scout officer and a disillusioned sergeant,
with hash-marks on his sleeve, were the point. The men
were echeloned back, right, and left with an automatic rifle
on each flank. In the centre marched the colonel, smoking,
to the horror of all, a cigar. Smoking was not done up there,
after dark. With him was the elegant French captain, who
appeared to be very gallantly resigned to it. The story
would, he reflected, amaze and delight his mess—if he ever
got back with it! These droll Americans! He must remember just what this colonel said: a type, *Nom de Dieu!* If only
he had not worn his new uniform—the cloth chosen by his
wife, you conceive——

The 75s flew with angry whines that arched across the
sky and smote with red and green flames along a line. . . .
There was a spatter of rifle-fire toward the right; flares
went up over the dark loom of the Bois; a certain violence
of machine-gun fire grew up and waxed to great volume,
but always to the right. Forward, where the shells were
breaking, there was nothing. . . .

The scout officer, leading, had out his canteen and wet

* 11.19 P.M.

his dry mouth. He was acutely conscious of his empty stomach. His mind dwelt yearningly on the mess-kit, freighted
nobly with monkey-meat and tomatoes, awaiting him in
the dependable Tommy's musette. "Hope to God nothing
happens to old Tommy!" The wheat caught at his ankles
and he hated war. Lord, how these night operations make
a man sweat! He went down a little gully and out of it, the
sergeant at his shoulder, breathing on his neck. That crater
—he visualized his map—it should be right yonder—two
of them. A hundred metres forward the last shells burst,
and he saw new dirt. Ahead, a spot darker than the dark;
he went up to it. Away on the right a flare soared, and
something gleamed dull in the black hole at his feet—a
round, deep helmet with the pale blur of a face under it; a
click, and the shadow of a movement there, and a little
flicker; a matter of split seconds; the scout officer had a
bayonet in his stomach, almost— Feldritter Kurt Iden,
Company 6 of the Margrave of Brandenburg Regiment
(this established later by brigade intelligence, on examina-
tion of the pay-book of the deceased), being on front post
with his squad, heard a noise hard on the cessation of the
shelling, and put out his neck. Dear God, shoot! Shoot
quickly!

The scout officer was conscious of a monstrous surge of
temper. He gathered his feet under him, and his hands
crooked like claws, and he hurled himself. In the same
breath there was a long, bright flash right under his arm,
and the mad crack of a Springfield. The disillusioned sergeant had estimated the situation, loosed off from the hip at
perhaps seven feet, and shot the German through the
throat. Too late to stop himself, the scout officer went head
first into the crater, his hands locking on something wet
and hairy, just the size to fill them; and presently he was at
the bottom of the crater, dirt in his mouth and a buzzing
in his head, strangling something that flopped and gurgled
and made remarkable noises under his hands. There were

explosions and people stepped hard on his back and legs. He
became sane again and realized that whatever it was it was
dead. He groped in his puttees for his knife, and cut off its
shoulder-straps and a button or two, and looted its bosom
of such papers as there were—there being details the complete scout officer must attend to. More explosions, and
voices bleating "Kamaraden!"—terribly anxious voices—in
his ear.

The disillusioned sergeant, a practical man, had ducked
into the crater right behind the scout officer. The raiding-
party in his rear had immediately fired their weapons in all
directions. A great many rifles on forward stabbed the dark
with sharp flame, and some of these were very near. The
sergeant tossed a grenade at the nearest; he had toted that
Frog citron grenade around for quite a while, somewhat
against his judgment; he now reflected that it was good
business—"grenades—I hope to spit in yo' mess-kit they are
—ask the man that used one—" It was good business, for it
fell fair in the other crater, thirty feet away, where the rest
of that front-post squad were beginning to react like the
brave German men they were. Two of these survived,
much shaken, and scuttled into the clever little tunnel that
connected them with the Feldritter's crater, emerging with
pacific cries at the sergeant's very feet. Being a man not
given to excitement, he accepted them alive, the while he
dragged the scout officer standing. "We got our prisoners,
sir. Le's beat it," he suggested. "Their lines is wakin' up,
sir. It's gonna be bad here——"

The colonel, as gallant a man as ever lived, but not fast,
barged into them. "Prisoners? Hey? How many? Two?
Excellent, by God! Give 'em here, young man!" and he
seized the unhappy Boches by their collars and shook them
violently. "Thought you'd start something, hey? Thought
you'd start something, hey?"

The scout officer now blew his whistle, the sergeant
shouted in a voice of brass, and the colonel made the kind

of remarks a colonel makes. The French captain, close
alongside, delightedly registered further events for narra-
tive. The raiding-party gathered itself—chaut-chaut gunners slamming out a final clip—and they all went back
across the wheat. It is related by truthful Marines there
present that every German in Von Boehn's army fired on
them as they went, but no two agree as to the manner of
their return. It is, however, established that the colonel,
bringing up the rear, halted about half-way over, drew his
hitherto virgin pistol, and wheeled around for a parting
shot—something in the nature of *un beau geste*. Seeing this,
the tall French captain, to his rear and left, drew his pistol
and wheeled also, imagining pursuit. The colonel—and to
this attest the scout officer and the sergeant—then shot the
Frenchman through the—as sea-going Marines say—stern-
sheets.

The scout officer and the sergeant got him back some
way, both filled with admiration at his language.

"If I had my time to do over, I'd learn this here Frog
habla," remarked the sergeant afterward. "I don't know
what the bird said, but it sure sounded noble. Ample, I
called it. Powerful ample."

By the time they stumbled through the nervous outposts
to their own place, the French captain had lapsed into
English. "As a wound, you perceive, it is good for a permis-
sion. But it is not a wound. It is an indignity! And, besides,
my new breeches! *Ah, Dieu de Dieu! Ce sale colonel-ci!*
What will my wife say! That one, she chose the cloth herself! *Tonnerre de canon!*"—and he sank into stricken
silence.

The raiding-party shook down in their several holes,
praising God, and went to sleep. The colonel, with his prisoners, received the compliments of Battalion Headquarters
and departed for brigade. The scout officer observed, to his
amazement, that they had been out of their lines less than
twenty minutes. "Where's the 49th?" he wanted to know

The scout officer and the sergeant got him back some way, both filled
with admiration at his language.

first. "Hell, Jim, they went up to the Bois right after the major sent for you. An' the 17th. We're moving Battalion Headquarters up there now. Get your people and come along. Attack or something."

After a very full night, the scout officer crawled and scuttled along the last tip of the Bois de Belleau, looking for a hole that a battalion runner told him about. "Seen the lootenant diggin' in just past that last Maxim gun, sir. Right at the nose of the woods where the big rocks is. There's about a dozen dead Heinies layin' by a big tree, all together. Can't miss it, sir." The scout officer had no desire to be moving in the cool of the morning, when all well-regulated people are asleep if possible, and if you moved here the old Boche had a way of sniping at you with 88s—that wicked, flat-trajectory Austrian gun—but he followed an urge that only Tommie could supply. "The damn slum will be cold, but two sardines and a piece of chocolate ain't filling!" He ducked low behind a rock as an 88 ripped by and burst on the shredded stump of a great tree; he tumbled into a shell-crater, atop an infantryman and three bloated Germans long dead; he scrambled out and fell over two lank cadavers in a shallow hole, who raised their heads and cursed him drowsily; and he came at last to a miserable shelter scooped in the lee of a rock. Here two long legs protruded from under a brown German blanket, and here he prodded and shook until the deplorable countenance of his brother officer emerged yawning.

"Say," demanded the scout officer, "you save my slum? Gimme my slum."

"Why, hello, Jim! Why didn't you come back, *like* you said you was? Where you been? You said you was comin' right back."

"Didn't you save me my monkey-meat? We went on a raid, damn it. I——"

"Raid? Raid? What raid?"

"War — sure — is — hell."

"Oh, we went over to Torcy. Gimme my monkey-meat."

"Well, you see, Jim—the fact is—well, we got moved up here right after you left, and they attacked from in here, an' we came on in after them. Just got to sleep——"

"I haven't had any sleep or any chow or anything—two sardines, by the bright face of God!—" The scout officer pounced upon a frowsy musette bag which the other had used for a pillow and jerked out a fire-blackened mess-kit. He wrenched the lid off and snarled horribly. "Empty, by God!"

His hands fell lax across his knees. He looked sadly over the blasted fields to Torcy, and he said, with the cold bitterness of a man who has tried it all and come to a final conclusion: "War—sure—is—hell."

SONGS

FOUR

"SWEET AD–O–LINE"

There were places like this down in the Touraine country, around the town Americans called St. Onion. Canals with poplars mirrored in them, where it was pleasant to loaf at the end of the day. The women were kindly and disposed to make friends; it is a pity that there were not enough to go around. They had, also, an eye for corporals and sergeants; the bored privates on the bank, sentimental souls, are singing "Sweet A-do-line . . ." or it may be something very different. The sergeant, a sensitive spirit, will presently see that they get some Extra Police Duty.

THE RHINE

THE BUGLES went while it was still as dark as the inside of a dog. There was swearing and sickly yellow candle-light in the billets, mean houses in a mean little Rhine-Province town, and the chow lines formed on the company galleys in an icy December rain. The rain pattered on helmets and mess-kits, and fell in slanting lines through the smoky circles of light where the cooking fires burned feebly. The faces of the Marines, as they filed out of the dark for food, were gray and frowsy. The cooks issued corn-bill hash, and dared any man to growl at the coffee. How the hell could it be boiled enough, with wet wood and very little of that—been up all night as it is— you sports just pull in your necks! The companies gulped their ration in sullen silence, rolled damp blankets into the prescribed pack, and when the bugles squawked assembly, they fell in without confusion or enthusiasm. Platoon sergeants, with flash-lights or lanterns, called the rolls; somewhere out in front, first-sergeants received the reports; officers clumped along the lines to their units, grumbling.— "All here, first sergeant?"—"Beg the capt'n's pardon— couldn't see you in the dark, sir—all present-counted-for, sir!—" "Nice day for a hike. Major says, goin' to the Rhine to-day. Eighteen or twenty kilomets—don't know exactly. Dam' such a war! I'd like the old kind, where you went into winter quarters—Brrr—" The captain pulled his collar around his ears.

159

Presently a bad-tempered drawling voice bayed "Squads right—march!—" There was a shuffle or hobnails in the mud, and the rattle of rifle-slings. The 1st Battalion of the 5th Marines took the road.

These German roads were all honestly metalled, but the inch or so of mud on the surface was like soup underfoot, and the overcoats soaked up the rain like blotting-paper. It was the kind of a morning with no line between night and daylight. The blackness, turned to gray, and, after a while, the major, on his horse, could look back and see the end of his column. The battalion, he reflected, was up to strength again. It hadn't been this large since it went to Blanc Mont, the end of September. He shut his eyes on that thought—a hundred and thirty men that came out, where a thousand went in—then replacements, and, after the Armistice, more replacements. Perhaps the quality was running down a little. The new chaps didn't seem as tall and broad as the old men, the tall, sunburnt leathernecks that went out the road from Meaux, toward Château-Thierry, in the spring. Odd, just six months since the spring. . . . But a few veterans and hard drilling between fights would keep the temper in an outfit . . . one remembered a phrase in an order of the division commander's—"The 2nd Division has never failed to impose its will upon the enemy. . . ." And to-day it crossed the German Rhine. . . . He swung out of his saddle and stood by the road to watch them pass; 1,200 men, helmets and rifles gleaming a little in the wet gray light. . . .

The road led eastward through a country of low hills, sodden in the rain. Untidy clouds sprawled on the crests and spilled wet filaments into the valleys. The land was all in cultivation, laid off in precise squares and oblongs; some newly ploughed, some sparsely green with turnips and rape. It looked ugly and ordered and sullenly prosperous. There was slow conversation in the column.

"—Anybody know where we goin' to-day?" "Damfino

The cooks issued corn-bill hash and dared any man to growl.

—naw—I did hear the skipper's orderly say we'd make the Rhine, some time—" "How far—" "Some guy was lookin' at a map at battalion. Said it was about thirty kilomets." "Jesus on his golden throne!—It's always 'bout thirty kilo-

A nice day for a hike.

mets in this dam' country—" "Yeh! But I remember one time it was twelve kilomets. The night we hiked up to Verdun, back last March. Had a Frawg guide—little shrimp wit' a forked beard. Ask him how far, all he'd say was: 'Dooz kilomets—dooz kilomets—' Hiked all night in the rain, like this, an' at daylight we come to a sign, wit' the

name of the place we're goin' to, an' it said 'Dooz kilomets'
—that guide, he let on that he was right su'prised—" But
there were very few men in the column who remembered
the hike to Verdun, in the early spring of 1918; in one
company eight, in another eleven; in the whole battalion
the barest handful. It had been a long road. The first way-
station was the Bois de Belleau; a lot of people stopped
there, and were there yet. And there were more, comfor-
tably rotting in the Forêt de Retz, south of Soissons. And
more yet, well dead around Blanc Mont. And a vast drift
of them back in hospitals. Men walked silent, remembering the old dead. . . . Twelve hundred men hiking to the
Rhine, and how many ghosts . . . The mist rolled around the
column.

"—You replacements never knew Corp'ral Snair, that
got bumped off at Soissons, dallyin' with a Maxim gun. He
was a musical cuss, an' he uster sing a song to the tune of
the 'Old Gray Mare—She Ain't What She Uster Be'—
somethin' like

> 'The U.S. flag will fly over Germany
> Less than a year from now——'

—and now it is, an' it's a pity he ain't here to see it—"
"Well, but he's restin' easy where he is—me, I'm cold as hell
an' this dam' drizzle is drainin' down my neck——"

There was nothing but the mist and the rain, and a mean,
cold little wind with a bite in it. North and south, from
the edge of Holland to the Metz gateway, all the armies
were marching. Ahead, just out of contact, went the German armies. The battalion passed a dense little wood of firs
—Christmas-tree woods, the battalion called them. This
clump showed unmistakably that it had been a camp; but
there was no litter; the Boche who bivouacked there had
left it neat and clean. Along the road in orderly piles were
some hundreds of the round German helmets, and parked
precisely in a cleared place, where horse-lines had been, was

a battery of 105 field howitzers. The old Boche was jettisoning what he didn't need. The battalion observed and was thoughtful.

"What about the ole Boche?—You think he was licked enough?" "No, I don't. That stuff back there, they laid it down under orders, like they do everything. It's stacked— it ain' just thrown away. An' look how they police up behind themselves—" "Yeh! Remember the other day, when we was advance-guard, we could see their rear-guard, sometimes—perfect order, an' all that—not like a defeated outfit, at all!" "Sure! I hope to spit in yo' mess-kit it ain't! An' those little towns back yonder, with the arches an' the flags and the welcome returnin' heroes stuff—none o' that was for us—" "They ain't licked enough. Look at this country—winter ploughin' done—everything ship-shape—no shell-holes—no trenches—no barb' wire—who in hell won this war, anyway?" "You said it. We oughter got up in here an' showed the old Boche what it was like, to have a war in his own yard." "Well, I've been in all of it, an' pers'nally I was glad when the shootin' stopped. I got me some sleep an' a full belly, an' a pair of new shoes—an' some fireman's underwear, too. An' I was right proud not to be killed. I ain't prepared to die—" "We know you ain't, sergeant—we know—" "Aw, belay that—I mean, I was glad, myself, but we oughter gone on—oughter 've finished it while we was at it. He wasn't licked enough, an' now he's goin' home like a peacock wit' seven tails——!"

This was the consensus of opinion, delivered with consideration in the rain. The replacements, especially those who had joined up after the Armistice, in Belgium, were savagely regretful. The chaps who had come in after the Champagne, and been among those present at one fight, were bloodthirsty, but to a lesser degree. Only the veterans were entirely calm.

The rain fell, the road grew heavier. The battalion, soaked and miserable, plodded on. They passed through

Men walked silent, remembering the old dead.

many villages, all alike; all ugly and without character. The houses were closed and shuttered. You saw few people, but you always had the feeling of eyes behind the shutters. One thick-bodied Boche, in uniform—an artilleryman, by his leather breeches—stood in the doorway of a house, smoking a porcelain pipe that hung to his knee. His face was set in a cast of hate. He stood and stared, and the battalion, passing, looked him over with respect.

"Understand a bird like that." "Yeh—he's honest. Those dam' Heinies in the billet last night, they made me sick. That fellow that talked English. Says he was glad his American frien's, present by agreement in the Rheinlan', to welcome—says that to me, an' would the Herr Soldier like a good cup of coffee?" "Dam' his remarks—how 'bout the coffee?" "Well, it tasted funny, but it was hot." "Old guy at our billet gave us some cognac. Hot stuff! He didn't let on, though.—You know those trick certif'cates a soldier's family gets in Germany?—Colored picture like a Croi' Guerre certif'cate, shows a fat, beer-drinkin'-Heinie angel standin' over a dead Boche—signed Wilhelm I. R.—you know. Well, this bird had six of them in his front room, all framed on the wall. I gathered they was his sons. Four bumped off at Verdun in 1916. One very recent—Soissons, July.—Wonder if we met that fella? He stood there an' looked at me while I was readin' them, an' he looked like a wolf. I don't blame him—. But howcome he gave us the cognac—?" Later the battalion learned that the Boche had orders to be hospitable. . . .

Toward noon the clouds lifted, and the rain slowed to a thin drizzle, although it did not stop. The battalion filed between hills toward a great valley, dimly seen. The hills towered over them, dark, menacing—"No wonder the ole Boche has such a mean disposition, livin' in a country like this—" The battalion came into a town with paved streets and trolley-cars and tall factory chimneys that did not smoke. Platoon commanders said it was Remagen; those towers to the right would be the bridge. There was a bridge, a great steel structure of high black arches. The battalion filed upon it. Under it black water flowed swiftly, with surges and eddies dimpled by the rain. High rocky hills came down out of the mist on the farther side.

"So this is the Rhine," remarked the battalion. "Hell!" A few files were interested. A lank Texan said: "I don't see much to make a fuss about. You boys ever see the Trinity in overflow time? Ten miles from bank to bank, in the McKenzie Bend country—why, we'd call this a creek down where I come from—" "Naw, it ain't much river—an' no more is your dam' Trinity! I was raised in Sent Louie—Ole Miss'sip', now—" 'Well, rivers in this country are mainly over-touted. That Marne, it wouldn't be much more'n a branch, down South. I never saw that there Vesle River, but a guy in the 32d Division, that was with me in Neuilly, he says you could mighty near jump across it." "Heard anything about chow?—Galleys went on ahead awhile ago—when do we eat——"

For four years no hostile troops with arms in their hands had seen this river; only sad files of prisoners had crossed it, under German guard. The battalion turned right on the eastern bank and went up the river, on a broad road between a cliff and the swift black water. There were many houses, a continuous town. It was past noon of a Friday, the 13th December, and the Boche school-children were out. They gathered to look at the passing column. The Marines eyed them keenly. These kids were different. They did not point or talk or cry out, after the manner of children. They stood in stolid groups, wooden-faced, with unwinking pale-blue eyes. The boys were nearly all in field-gray uniform cloth—cut down, perhaps, from the cast-off clothes of an elder. Some of them wore boots and round soldier-caps. They carried books and lunch-boxes, knapsack fashion, on their shoulders.—"Look, will you—that kid there ain't more'n a yearlin', and they've got him in heavy

One thick-bodied Boche. . . . His face in a caste of hate.

They stood in stolid groups, wooden-faced.

marchin' order a'ready!" "Yeh,—they start 'em early—
that's howcome they're the way they are—these Boche."
There were round-faced little girls with straw-colored
braids, in cloaks. They did not look poorly fed, like the
waxen-faced children the battalion remembered in France.
And at every corner there were more of them. The battalion was impressed.—"Say—you see all those kids—all
those little square-heads! Hundreds of 'em, I'll swear!
Something's got to be done about these people. I tell you,
these Boche are danger-ous! They have too many children——"

The 1st Battalion of the Rhine — 5th Marines took the road.